CH01507268

WE GOT ZOMBIES ON THE LAWN AGAIN, MA

DONNIE SMITH

Dedicated to Kathy,
Who always believed.

Hear the praise for Ax Handel, true hometown hero!

"That boy is disturbingly comfortable around those dead . . . *things*. They're like the zombie sons we never wanted."

—Dor Handel, Axel's mother

"He told me he sees the world through zombie-colored glasses. Whatever. At least he's finally got some friends."

—Zenobia Paccorelli, Axel's ex-girlfriend

"I don't owe you $200. Wait! Don't do that—put that away! Tell you what: I'll pay you back if you can take me down in less than twelve seconds."   *—Juan Anderson, Axel's imperfect father*

"I want you to know that if this troubled town had ten more just like him, that'd give us eleven."

—unfunny old dude outside Berta's Bait Shop

"One time we waited like, six hours to get our pizza, but it never came, dude. So we booked over to Axel's house, and he was all, 'Why are you at my house? It's three o'clock in the morning! Next time, call in your order, robobakers.' We gave him a thirty-dollar tip."   *—this one stoner dude named Hash*

"All I'm going to say is I had nothing to do with his stupid book! Why are you following me? Are you recording this? No, I don't know anything about his zombies. He clowned around in class all the time, did he tell you that? What? I'm not answering that. What does that have to do with Ax Handel? Listen, I'm not going out with you, I don't care how many men you've killed. Are you a real reporter?"

—Mrs. Clarkson, Axel's high school writing teacher

FOREWORD

I was twelve when I first saw George Romero's classic *Night of the Living Dead*. I sat alone in my darkened bedroom as eerie gray light oozed from the little thirteen-inch Philco, inexorably transfixing me while casting sinister shadows across my Led Zeppelin posters on the walls. And my mind spun.

That film made quite an impression on me and before long, zombie movies became a favorite of mine. There's something about dead people coming back to life to torment and eat the living that I find deeply troubling . . . and funny. The more I watched, the more I questioned their motives. The part that's never really made sense to me is their appetite for live brains. I just don't get it. I mean, it's hard to believe zombies could be that spiteful—and particular when it comes to their diet.

Think about it: if you died and were reanimated, what would you desire more than anything? A second chance to do right by your loved ones and society in general? How about another shot at scoring that game-winning goal? Nah, you'd bite down on some guy's head and ruin his day. Wait, really?

After a while, I started thinking that maybe Hollywood got it all wrong. Perhaps not all zombies are into cannibalism and pissing themselves. And maybe—just maybe—there are people out there who don't view zombies as loathsome creatures. Instead, they see unproductive, misplaced citizens. So, what if those enlightened innovators tapped into their newfound and abundant zombie resources in order to improve their world?

Ax Handel happens to be one of those forward thinkers. He's no superman, he's just a guy who takes lemons and makes zombie-ade.

Donnie Smith

1

I NEVER SAID IT WAS PERFECT

I know what you're thinking: "Hey, Ax, is this book about me?"

Answer: yes.

That is, if you're a zombie. Because if you are, then yeah, it's about you. If you're not, then you have nothing to worry about—your secret's safe with me.

Ever since ninth grade, when my girlfriend, Zenobia, told me she was going to be a psychologist and that I should keep a diary, I've been writing stuff down in notebooks. Everything you read in this book is from junk I wrote in my first zombie notebook, and most of it has to do with the same thing: unwashed and unwanted houseguests. It's all basically in order, because if it wasn't that'd just be confusing and stupid. If you notice that sometimes there's quite a bit of space and time between events, it's because nothing much happened in the middle, so I left out those parts because I couldn't think of nothing. The thing is, our yard fills up with zombies every day, so that's pretty much the main deal.

Oh, by the way, you ever notice how a lot of books start out the same way? I mean, say you're standing there in the library—I know it sounds crazy: you in the library? What are you doing, looking for a place to hide? Okay, let's say you are. Suppose you're running from that crazy chick—you know the one—and you end up in the library. While you're crouching silently behind the overstuffed shelves, you've got one eye on the door and the other on all those unread books. Man, they've got a lot of books, don't they? Do you think there's like, one guy who might've read all those books? Maybe, I don't know.

Anyway, the next thing you know, a wicked cramp starts donkey-choking the fat part of your thigh, forcing you to stand up and stretch that bad boy. While you're up, you begin looking closer at some of the titles, and then you see a book that looks like it could be interesting. Eagerly, you pull it out, and as you're checking out the picture on the cover, it reminds you of that one time when you almost read a book.

When you open it up to the first page, you're obviously wondering if there's any porn in it. Too bad though, because it begins a lot like that other book you almost read, sort of like "The gentlest of misty morning breezes caressed the downy meadow as the buttercup sun generously shared its life-giving warmth . . ." or something dull and long-winded like that, right? Then, immediately following that completely forgettable line are thirty-six overly descriptive paragraphs of some place you don't give a shit about. Doesn't it seem like there are just way too many books that begin that way?

Well, this is another one.

Only, this one starts out different. And speaking of zombies, I have to deal with them on a day-to-day, so that's in here too. Problem is, there are so many things people don't know about zombies somebody should write a book about it. I remember one day I got into a discussion with Ma about zombies and she wasn't that much help.

Ma," I said, "question: didn't you tell me once that church is no place for a zombie? Well, then, what the hell was that scraggly, boozer-looking zombie doing coming out of the confessional at St. Mary's yesterday afternoon? You wanna explain that one, Miss Churchy-shoes?"

"Zombies have sins too, Axel," she said matter-of-factly.

"You said zombies don't go to church."

"They do if they've sinned."

"What sin could a zombie commit?"

That got her worked up. "Are you kidding me? Zombies do all kinds of nasty shit. And you can bet the Lord ain't too happy about it, either."

"So Father Bateman is taking confessions from the zombies now?"

"I doubt it, son. I mean, think about it. If you were a priest, and a zombie came to you and confessed that he'd been doing crazy zombie shit, what would you say?"

"I'd have to think of something, I guess," I said.

"Like what? Are you going to tell him to say ten Our Fathers and stop eating the neighbors?"

"Would that work? Or should I talk to Father Bateman first?"

"Would you absolve him?"

"I think I would have to, if I'm a priest and all. But before I do that, I'll check with Father Bateman—he'll know what I should do."

"It won't matter. The zombie has already died and been judged once. He doesn't get a do-over—that's double jeopardy."

I was puzzled.

"So what do you say to him after he's confessed all his sins and shit, and he wants absolution? Do you tell him there's no need to confess anymore, because it won't do any good? Do you tell him he just has to go with the first verdict, whatever that was? Hey, maybe you could ask him how that judging thing went the first time around after he died—I'd like to know about that."

"What?" Ma looked confused and annoyed.

"You know, did St. Peter let him in or what? How did that work? Did he have to take a test first? What was his score? Oh, hey, is there a way to study for it? And then—wait a minute! If he did pass his test and got through the pearly gates, why is he back here? What about that? If somebody has already been let into heaven, can he just come back to earth as a zombie and do whatever he wants? And if you do, do you get punished for committing zombie acts? Do they give you the boot, so that after you're done being a zombie you go straight to hell?"

"Jeez, Axel, are you done? That was like, fifty questions."

"Not just questions, Ma. Questions without answers."

"I'll tell you what: if you come back as a zombie and want to confess to me, go ahead. But I won't be listening."

That was the day Ma taught me not to ask her questions about stuff.

Okay, let's get back in the room. Maybe my writing isn't so great—not my fault. Talk to Mrs. Clarkson about that, she was my writing teacher in ninth and tenth grade. Sure, there were times when I was putting this together that I thought about trying harder to write right. Problem is, they have a zillion rules and twice as many exceptions, and I can't remember them all. And even if I did, half of them seem contradictory and nobody agrees on the grammar stuff anyway.

So I just wrote it the way I talk, which is what one of my other teachers a long time ago told me to do. Instead of trying to be technically correct, I used my own speech patterns and idioms and whatnot. That's the best I can do.

Don't blame me if I chose the wrong words or my transistors aren't the smoothest—I'm a product of the public educational system, so take it up with them. If you want the perfect zombie book, maybe you could take a writing class from Ernest Shakespeare and have him write it for you. Problem is, you'll need to have a few homeless zombies hanging around, and since they only seem to contemplate in my yard, you'll probably have to leave out all the good stuff about zombies. So let's just keep it the way it is. Besides, hearing a good story is in the eye of the beholder, right?

Anyway, yeah, they told me not to use slang or cuss words, but sometimes you just gotta—you know what I'm talkin' about, bro! Ha-ha! If it bothers you that much, close your eyes when you read those parts.

Cripes, what would you like me to do, hire 1,000 sharp-dressed monkeys to write 1,000 stories about a sincere zombie monkey and then choose the most righteous monkey to tell my story? That's the stupidest idea I ever heard. Plus, I don't know nothing about no zombie monkey, so I don't even know what you're talking about.

All right, these are some of the chronicles that occurred over the last year. If you're not too scared, leave the lights off. Or on . . . if you dare. And you should know, there's a lot of important zombie stuff in here they were afraid to teach you in school, so think of these stories as the zombie teachers you never had but always wanted.

For example, there was this guy in my study hall last year named Sparky, who, although he wasn't a teacher and he never personally knew any zombies, dressed up like a zombie for Halloween once. He looked really real and it paid off big time. That year he got more candy than anybody. His secret? He stole his little brother's allowance and blew it all on candy fangs and wax lips.

Also, I remember Ma once told me there's something to be learned from every experience, no matter how sucky it is. And I say that those who do not learn from history probably had Mr. Wingate in tenth grade, who's just a boring ass.

2
A TYPICAL FAMILY

My name is Ax Handel, and I live with zombies.

You ever have festering, moaning demons in your yard? I can tell you firsthand it gets to be real aggravating. But after you accept it, just like you've accepted your Uncle Daxton's not-so-secret mannequin perversions, you milk it for all it's worth. Because, just like death and the circus (and even Uncle Daxton's shady parole officer), zombies only come around once in a lifetime, so it's smart to make the best of it.

The undead are uncomplicated—not a lot of moving parts there. I didn't realize that at first, but I had learned way back in second grade that it helps to know your enemy, so I set up tactical zombie surveillance immediately. Sitting in a tree by the house, I made notes of their basic movements: shamble, attack, shamble. It took me a solid month to compile that data . . . hold on, now that I think about it, instead of listening to tunes and playing *Words with Friends*, I could have figured that out in the first ten minutes. Still, I guess it needed to be done; I mean, I don't want to be like my Uncle Rotor, who's a blind airplane pilot and flies by feel—that's not my style.

Learning how to defend myself against zombies was another matter entirely. It's not like they teach you that stuff in school, which they don't, by the way. When I first faced a horde of those filthy snackers, I was a little tense because I didn't know how to ride the bull, as they say. As time went by, it got easier. Then it got harder. Then it was time for supper.

I guess I'm not too scared of them cuz I can handle myself, whereas they have trouble in that area. I mean, they don't even bother staying in shape. Have you ever seen a zombie work out? Ever stand in line, patiently waiting for a zombie to finish up on the leg press machine? Me neither, so how do they expect to be successful? Their greatest strength is intimidation, and that can take you only so far. And their biggest weakness is lack of strength, which seems to work against them.

Luckily for me, we had a lot of dickheads in my high school, because that helped keep my fighting skills sharp. That, along with Dad training me has my fist biceps peaking at the right time; I try to keep them in top fighting condition. And speaking of fist power, it's a scientific fact that my fist often strikes a deserving face willfully and with astonishing force. You know how they say an angry man with nothing to live for and no fear of dying is the most dangerous creature of all? Wrong—my fist is.

Also, my fists were taught at an early age to destroy everything in their path—just ask James "The Mouth" Keegan about that. Remember that day in church, Jimbag? It was right after Bible school. We were in third grade and you ate it big time, ending up sprawled under the altar. Get thee behind me, Jimmy! Sister Andrea, can we get a late checkout for "The Mouth," please? Looks like he's gonna miss Confession.

After graduating from high school last year, I decided to shape up a little and try to make something of myself. I've always had a job, mostly delivering pizzas, and now I'm working extra hard and saving up my money. I don't hafta ask my folks for cash anymore, so I'm set. Only thing is, nowadays I have to deal with zombies, and they have a way of messing up my plans. Still, I'm learning that if you spin it just right, you can keep the zombies in their place and profit from it.

Except for Zenobia (my ex), my friends are dinks. Most of them think I'm nuts, or on drugs. Or both. Or neither. I decided not to talk to them about zombies anymore—all they do is laugh their stupid asses off and toss their empties at me. They even started calling me Mystery Mike behind my back, which I don't get because he was that weird, crooked-smile janitor dude at school who never tied his bootlaces.

So that's why they're my best friends and I hate them. Besides, being a bunch of stoners mostly, what would they know? And like my dad says, you can't blame kids for being rotten—you need to spread the credit around, to their parents and teachers.

Too bad for them, but none of my friends really get me. Ma gets me. One time when we were vacuuming up spiders in the basement, she looked at me and said, "Axel, if we were living on the moon, and you weren't my son, we might be neighbors. That's right, neighbors on the moon." That made me smile; I'm pretty sure we're riding the same wave.

I got bigger problems than dink friends anyway. I know what I know, and what I know nobody should have to know. It can be a really real problem for my family, cuz sometimes we don't even know, and we're the ones who usually know. Handling the zombie situation properly is challenging at times, and it was especially hard at first, but we take care of business when we need to.

As I said, I'm Ax Handel. My mom is Doris Handel. And my dad is—you guessed it—Juan Anderson.

Ma's been around and she's a tough cookie who'll take you to knuckle junction if you look at her—she hates to be looked at. And Dad, well, he's the hammer *and* the nail; he goes by Jak for short, and he's a mad bastard.

It was Ma who raised me the most because after I was born Dad prioritized, and he put us near the bottom of his list. He was hardly ever home. I mean, he came around once in a while and he taught me how to fight, but that was about all. It worked out though, cuz Ma knows what she's doing, and I don't feel like I missed much.

At five-six and weighing in around one-forty, she's no pushover. Fifty-some years old and tough as nails, she wears her blond hair chopped to her shoulders, sometimes with black dye streaked in it, which looks okay, I guess. She's usually casual, so you almost always see her in tie-dyed T-shirts, black jeans, and black motorcycle boots.

Growing up in the seventies, she was a runaway who worked as a roadie for some headbanger bands in LA back in the day, which means she's heavily into old metal: Misfits, Maiden, Priest, Sabbath. She likes pizza & root beer and *The Munsters*—but hey, who doesn't?

Mess with Ma, get your jaw broken. Period. She once punched out a drunk who was rude to her. Afterward, he bitterly mumbled through broken teeth that she hit like a girl. Looking down at him, she said, "If you tried a little harder, you could too," and took out his last good tooth.

Ma takes absolutely nothing from nobody, and she doesn't care about the opinions of others or what people think of her. When it comes to snooty posers, she scoffs, "They're vipers, and you can't let them bamboozle you. They may think they're special, but do you really think God has us ranked, and he put them a notch higher than me?" Ma makes a good point regarding artificial elitism.

She gave up smoking a few years ago—cuz of the tar and Dentyne, probably—so now she's into the juicy bubblegum cigarettes. Those things are gnarly good. Plus, when you puff on them, tiny wisps of candy smoke come out, so that's a bonus. She's a pretty good mom, and I guess that makes me lucky. And while she's usually fair and flexible, you'd better not get too cheeky because that's the quickest path to danger. Also, don't brody any of her bubblegum cigs cuz she'll flip, and while she's chasing you out the back door with a hammer she's screaming that you're grounded for life.

Being a lifetime heavy metal banger, Ma cranks a tune like nobody. That was a bit much for the square neighbors at our old place, who whined about it at first. But like a natural diplomat, Ma got them all together and ironed out a compromise. She proposed that they let her play loud music only when she really needed it (meaning those times when they were pissing her off, but she didn't say it like that), and in turn, she would install their home theater systems and nuke-boost the bass for a small fee. They quickly went along with it, mainly because they understood that high-decibel heavy metal music was Ma's only means of venting without erupting into uncontrollable violence and kicking all their complaining asses.

Now her hearing is starting to go from all those years of standing in front of a wall of speakers at infinity concerts, so sometimes I gotta yell to make myself heard, even when she's an inch away. Other times her hearing is real good and she gets all pissed off when she hears things.

Like one time I was cranking high-voltage Misfits in my room cuz I was downstoked about getting fired from The Pizza Krust. I was hoping that my boss, Prince Mmbobo, also known as the Great Iowa Falsifier, was going to hire me back, but in the meantime, I was pretty bummed. So I turned up my music. At first, the chainsawing guitars didn't help me feel too optimistic, so I cranked it up to nine—Ma taught me never to roll it to ten, unless you feel like rebuilding your speakers after you crack the drivers. When my sub starting shaking the shit off my shelf was about the time Ma flung open my door and started in on me.

"Axel, turn down the music!" She wasn't really mad; she'd probably just been trying to watch TV or something.

"What, Ma?" I yelled to make myself heard.

"The music is too loud, Axel!"

"What?"

She grimaced. "Turn down the music!"

"Ma, I can't hear you—the music's too loud!"

That's when she marched up to me in her black Scorpions T-shirt until she was within half an inch from my face. She was wearing that look that said there was maybe one second left in my life. I wisely spun around on my bed and shut down the tunes.

"You don't have to yell, Ma. You could just ask me nice," I muttered.

She tilted her head meaningfully and looked at me for a second before saying, "Axel, I'm always nice to you, jackass."

That's the way Ma is and that's how it is.

Dad, who is a couple years older than Ma, is about six feet two, 230 pounds, and he'll kick your ass. He keeps his hair very black and thick, and it's always slicked back with *mucho* oil. His long sideburns bring to mind a murderous young Elvis, and he possesses slick fashion instincts. He's a regular popinjay, at least that's what he always tells me. And, like Ma, he always wears shiny black biker boots.

Dad's made his mark in the world. He's been a schoolteacher, bouncer, correctional officer, security guard, and house painter. And I think that as a result of all those low-paying, no-respect, working-with-overpaid-pricks jobs, he's a well-equipped and mean son of a bitch who hates people. Let's face it, he's had to put up with a lot of tools who walk around with an inflated sense of importance—you know, natural dicks. As an educator, he was so good it really pissed off the teachers who were just mailing it in, and they let him know it. He once said that when Neil Young sang he "don't feel like Satan but I am to them" Dad knew Neil was talking about him.

Egomaniacs, including lazy-ass school principals, self-loving politicians, authoritative teachers, and pompous administrators are Dad's primary nemeses. He's fond of saying, "Those are the laziest, most ill-informed, destructive people on the globe. And their addiction to artificial authority has no limits. There's no accountability, and maintaining a position of influence in which they hold court over the most easily dominated segments of society—including children—serves to whet their thinly veiled perpetual drive to better their own situation—at the expense of their decidedly voiceless constituents."

Whatever you do, when you're around Dad don't ever mention one of those people, because they've scroogled him so many times he'll give your ear a mouthful. And you better hope you're not in a restaurant, because he'll look around at all the tables for somebody who looks like the person you just mentioned. Then the first thing he'll do is walk over and stand next to him, giving him the death eye. When the dope asks him what his problem is, Dad picks up the guy's plate and smashes the mashed potatoes and steak gristle into his bearded face while whacking him to the floor with an overhand right. Now the guy is out cold and covered with gravy while Dad's getting thrown out and once again I have to pay for the whole dinner just because I said the actor on that old *Twilight Zone* episode about the world ending talked just like Dad's old boss.

Other than that, he's always calm, unless he completely loses it, which happens all the time. Especially when somebody provokes him. Then, under the best of circumstances, you might be able to calm him down with orange soda and fortune cookies, unless he's in front of the TV watching the New York Rangers lose again; then you're better off walking away.

He only has one child—me—and over the last few years we've pretty much become best friends, but he won't eat cold pizza, which is obvious proof that you can't teach old tricks to a new dog. And the thing is, sometimes I don't even know which dog he is.

One day we were eating double cheeseburgers at Hamburger Pants when he leaned in toward me and said, "Axel, I'm a risk taker. My friends call me Rock."

I hadn't heard that before. "Because you're steady as a rock, and that makes you strong enough to take crazy chances?" I asked.

He sniffed real serious-like. "No, because I like rock music."

That's my dad—now he's Rock Anderson. News to me.

A few days later, we were working on my car when he put down the plug wrench and said confidently, "Ax, anytime you need somebody dusted, you call me—no questions asked. In lockup they called me Duster."

I hesitated before eyeing him warily. "Because you'd dust anybody, anytime, just like that?"

"No, because I drove a flame-orange '76 Plymouth Duster with sweet glass packs that sounded wicked bad from two blocks away. Back then I was known as The Rumbler."

"Because your car sounded so cool?" I asked, but I don't know why.

"No, because I'd rumble with anybody anytime—I had a bad temper. Growing up, the neighbors called me Short Fuse."

He was glaring at me menacingly, as if trying to prove it.

"Because you blew their shit up?" I wasn't going to fall for it again.

"Exactly. So don't forget it, *Martillo*."

He was no-nonsense, like he wanted to fight somebody. Or blow up their shit. Or fight them while blowing up their shit.

"I won't, Dad."

But I didn't laugh or nothing because the unsmiling look on his face told me he was serious. And part psycho.

As far as our family background, Dad's Latino and Ma's a bit of a Polish pirate, and that makes me both. Back when I was a kid Dad called me a hell razor, but only until I was in the seventh grade. Then one day during lunch period, I gave a thumper to the eighth-grade bully. I got suspended, but that's when my parents started calling me *Polski Martillo*, which transmits in English to the "Polish Hammer." Dad was so proud that his son took care of business he decided to go to the principal and bawl her out for not giving me an award.

For some reason, before he left the house that day Dad said something about wanting a piece of the kid's father, which I didn't understand. I think it was because he doesn't like feeling left out. Anyway, I didn't find out till later if Dad got his hands on the guy. Ma held off supper for a while, but we finally ate without him. Then, later that night when I came out of my room to get some Hawaiian Punch, Dad was sitting at the kitchen table. He gave me a smug grin, and I noticed he was eating corn pancakes topped with cinnamon applesauce—his victory meal.

Dad and me are about the same size, except his fist is bigger and has more miles on it while I have blond hair. Speaking of hair, I don't go to the Kwik Kut anymore because, even though those haircutting girls are nice, they never listen to me and always cut my hair wrong. They style it the way *they* want to and say, "It looks nice like this," which makes me just want to take the electric clippers to them a little. But hey, it's only hair, right? And just because it's only hair, is that any reason to hate them? Yes.

So from now on Ma or my old girlfriend, Zenobia, cuts it cuz they listen to me when I say keep it out of my eyes, your choice on the sides, and whatever in the back. So that problem is now solved and my hair is happy.

Here's something you'll like: I have one brown eye and one green eye. Hardly anyone notices, so it's no biggie. Plus, I'm pretty sure it helps me see more colors. Nobody knows how it happened, but there's not a lot I can do about it, so there you go. Does that make me a bad person? Sometimes.

But I'm not going to grouse about it. I mean, you're either a good person or a bad person, right? You can't be anything else. Or, maybe you could be somebody who's good sometimes and bad sometimes, like my Uncle Mickey; but I've learned that, just to be safe, you shouldn't go near Uncle Mickey, cuz he smells like a damn *rata de al cantarilla*—sewer rat!

Also, I like lifting weights—not to show off or anything. I don't wear boys' extra-small shirts to make myself look big like some of those tubers at the gym. It's just something Dad started me on in junior high school for hockey and fighting, and I liked the way it made me feel. Like, stronger or something. Probably from the weights. Anyway, if you know somebody who needs a beating and wants to lock up for a couple rounds, let's do it. I fear no mortal, alive or dead.

I started working at The Pizza Krust restaurant when I was fifteen, and it's an okay job. I mean, it's helped me pay off my car loan and it keeps me in scratch, so there's that. Plus, my bosses are okay and I don't hate the work too much. When I first started there, I was a pizza maker, which was hard at first. But then it got pretty cool, because we have this big sixteen-square-foot window between the customers and the pizza-making counter, and sometimes it feels like you're onstage.

Usually, you get some kids or maybe a cute girl standing there on the other side of the window watching you make pizzas. So you act all important like you're Luigi, professional pizza guy from Italy. Pretty soon, you're flying around cranking out pizzas at light speed because you think you're cool, and because you know that's what the spectators came to see.

Sometimes when you notice a bunch of little kids with their chubby faces mooshed up against the glass, you get carried away and occasionally flip a wet pepperoni up at them. It's funny because they forget about the glass and jump back, away from the dangerous flying pizza topping. Then they see the spicy projectile stuck to the other side of the glass and they giggle hysterically. You don't realize it but you're snickering too, and after a couple minutes the window is so coated with sticky pepperoni discs you can't see their faces. That's when you're hoping the Mikes don't decide to come out of the cave to check up on you.

The Mikes are three college guys who manage the place for Mmbobo. They all have the same first name but they're not related. And for the most part, they're pretty cool about working with a bunch of smart-ass teenagers. Only two of the Mikes are ever on duty at a time, but when they're supposed to be managing us, they're usually in the cave at the back of the building, which is actually the office. Normally, they stay back there all night YouTubing or watching porn, so we hardly ever see them. They're great bosses.

Mostly, I deliver pizzas now, and once in a while Prince Mmbobo, the owner, fires me to make himself feel better. I guess I don't mind anymore because he always hires me back. It used to make me mad, but Ma helped me understand that it's the only way he knows how to manage, and it's never for a good reason. Usually, he's bent up about the crew costing him money, or the crew screwing around too much, or the crew dipping into the register, or that time he caught the crew in the cooler guzzling down the root beer, or something stupid like that. Then, he sees me and my long hair and rebel eye colors and fires me. Zenobia says I should sue him, but I like him—and the Mikes—and the job pays the bills so it's cool for now.

One thing I don't understand is why Mmbobo lies. When I first met him, he was evasive and jittery, and he wouldn't look me in the eye. And since I could hardly understand what he was saying because I wasn't listening and because of his thick foreign accent, I asked him where he was from. He suddenly stiffened up and his eyes got wide. Standing there frozen for a few seconds, he abruptly burst into a suspiciously fake smile and said he was from Iowa, nodding excitedly while eagerly showing lots of teeth.

I wasn't sure I'd heard him right, so I asked, "Iowa? Like Iowa in the Caribbean? Or the Iowa in Africa, where they don't speak English?"

He stared at me for a long second before making a phony grimace as if he was offended. He looked down and started fiddling nervously with some papers on his desk, mumbling that he was born and raised in Iowa, which, when he said it, sounded like *Eye-ew-oh*, which isn't even close.

When I told him my previous job was with the Immigration Department and I was going to look him up in our files, he got skittish and bumped up my salary—and I hadn't even started working there yet! I looked him straight in the eye and told him he can live with his lies, but one day I would defeat him and take over his pizza empire, which I didn't really mean, but in that moment I was channeling Lt. Jim Dangle. He screamed at me to get the hell out of his office, which I did, but only after snagging all the black jelly beans out of his candy jar.

Moving on, the other main person in my life is Zenobia

Paccorelli, who's a wild spitfire. At first, she reminded me of my seventh-grade art teacher, who I had a major crush on until I found out she was a succubus. And a guy. Zenobia's neither, but sometimes she comes close to being a demon. You might say she's more like a hateful mime, but replace the miming part with aggressive bad-mouthing.

Standing fairly tall, she's got a nice frame and the mindset of a truck driver who won't pay alimony. Plus, she will not back down from anyone. Sound familiar? Yup, she's a younger, crazier Ma. And even though she's only a year older than me and practically raised herself with nothing but a badass attitude and a little help from her grandma, who she lives with, she thinks she can push me around.

Anyway, I don't know what happened to Zenobia's parents, and she won't tell me, so I feel a little sad for her. Also, guess what? You got it—she's essentially Ma's best friend. Those two are sisters from hell at times, meaning when you've crossed them. Then you need to head for the door immediately. That's a gift you don't want under your Christmas tree.

I first got to know Zenobia through her habitual stalking. That's right, she followed me around for like, two months in junior high school. It was weird, and funny. Everywhere I went, there she was; every day, all the time, her dark, sinister eyes hiding behind silky black bangs. I knew she had an edge to her, what with anger issues and a general feeling of needing to kick someone's ass, and that made me somewhat nervous. But she was cute and I knew she was a tough chick, which I liked.

One day I came out of the boys' gym locker room and she was standing there wearing dark shades and a long-sleeved Iron Maiden T-shirt while chewing gum and blowing big bubbles. She reminded me of one those hard biker chicks from the fifties.

Her eyes were locked on mine and she was all, "You wear

black every day. Why do you always wear black?" in a husky, accusing voice.

Of course, my answer was, "Isn't that a little stalky?"

But, I admired her persistence and after a while I kind of fell for her.

For the next five years or so, Zenobia was my girlfriend. But that ended last year; now she's sort of my friend. I guess it's because sometimes when we were dating I'd punk her a little cuz I thought it was funny, and a few months ago she'd finally had enough and told me to get lost. At first, it didn't bother me as much as it should have, I suppose. But a couple weeks later, I started thinking about her and me a lot, and what went wrong. That's when I figured out the problem: I was a dink.

So, I trucked over to her place and told her what I had learned about myself. She didn't say anything but just glared silently at me. Then I walked away, leaving her standing there in the doorway, not too mad at me anymore, I think. I felt a lot better after that because, although I didn't ask anything from her—I figured she would never take me back anyway—I really wanted to tell her what I had realized.

She surprised me by coming over the next day, and we talked about some junk and stuff. Ever since then, we're pretty good, except for her simmering hatred of me. I suppose it's like one of Ma's old hippie expressions: "If you love something, let it go; if it comes back to haunt you, it wants revenge." That may be, because Zenobia's habitually mean to me now. She's been screwed over a lot, and I know I'm one of the reasons for her bombastic temperament, so I guess I got it coming. The only thing I can do now is wait her out.

She's trying hard to put some stuff behind her, like when she quit working at The Pizza Krust because Mmbobo fired her too many times. She once told me that she woke up every morning for an entire week with severe hand cramps from strangling Mmbobo all night in her dreams. Now she angrily works at Hamburger Pants and goes to the community college.

Ma says I'm a lot like Zenobia because I've got a short fuse. I don't know about that, but if you push me, you'll get the boots—nobody gets second or third chances with me. But it's not like I'm a live wire or anything; heck, I wake up every day in a good mood and I don't go around looking for trouble. Just don't provoke me, that's all. We all need to be nice to each other, and if you're not nice, then you're getting the thunder, and I'm bringing it into your living room. I've sort of learned to be that way. Growing up with a crazed hippie for a mother and a cynical hard-ass for a father will do that, I suppose.

Getting back to Zenobia, that girl can be a real puzzle. I mean, it's like this. After ZombieMania III in my backyard last August, I was pretty beat up and sore. It was an all-night fight show I put on for some of the neighborhood kids, and I must have tuned up thirty-five zombies—the rowdy fans got their money's worth that night! However, a few of the better zombie fighters did manage to get in some shots on me, and by the time the sun came up, my ribs and neck were hurting.

The show lasted about eight hours, and when it was all over, I crawled into my Mustang and headed over to Zenobia's house because—like a bad former girlfriend—she never bothered to show up for the event and I had to see what her deal was.

Shredding white-hot Misfits tunes all the way over there nearly tore up my rear speakers, but I didn't care; I needed to relax. When I arrived on Zenobia's porch ten minutes later, it must have been about seven in the morning. She came to the door in her black karate pajamas, which had *WHEN I DIE I'M HAUNTING YOU FIRST* in bright blood-red letters across the front. Without saying a word, she eyed me up and down a few times. Then she scowled a little and turned around with her messed-up coal-black hair and shuffled tiredly back into the house. Ever so cautiously, I followed her in.

Keeping a safe distance, I looked at the back of her head and boldly said, "Hi, Z. You're looking good. *Por favor présteme su animal crackers*—Please lend me your animal crackers," in a polite, lilting voice. I was still mad at her, but I was hoping she had some snacks stashed away because, strangely, the smell of early morning cinnamon had my belly rumbling.

"No," she answered without turning around before plopping lazily into the big, soft rocking chair. From there she watched me with half-open eyes.

There were no lights on, with the exception of seven or eight orange candles burning around the perimeter of the living room. It was eerily shadowy, and the flickering candles gave off a stomach-growling cinnamon and pumpkin pie scent. The headache in my neck was really kicking in, so I gently eased down onto the edge of the seven-foot tan sofa across the room from the scary girl. Uncomfortably, I peeked over and saw her eyeing me uncertainly while slowly rocking in her chair, one leg crossed under the other, moving rhythmically back and forth like a sober, resentful ass-kicking pendulum about to fall off the wagon.

Working up my courage, I jumped right in and began talking excitedly about the important fighting jamboree that had just ended.

"There were probably seven or maybe eight kids there watching, so don't feel sad that you weren't part of the crowd," I said and paused, waiting for a reaction that didn't come. "Yeah, it's too bad you missed it. I wouldn't say I got injured or anything like that, maybe just a sore neck or something. There's nothing you can do about it anyway." I rubbed the back of my neck, where the skull meets the muscle.

Her expression was unreadable and never changed as she

listened indifferently. Not surprisingly, I guess, she didn't even ask how I did. So I didn't bother to tell her I went a robust 35-0, which I was pretty proud of.

Pulling her other leg up and under, she stopped rocking and sat cross-legged and stiffly upright like that one Buddha dude—but not chubby or bald, just mean. Sitting motionlessly, it looked like she was meditating, or gauging the atmosphere of the underworld for signs of challengers to her throne. With the sinister, red-orange reflection of the surrounding candlewicks dancing devilishly in her black eyes, I thought for a minute that maybe she was a witch.

But then, no, it was just Z, sitting there calmly, eating a bag of tortilla chips. And not sharing.

"Hey, where'd you get those? Are they macho cheese?" I asked, my stomach yowling. I leaned forward a little, studying the bag. "Can I have the folded-over ones?"

"There are no folded-over ones," she monotoned.

"Come on, I just want the foldovers."

"Why?" she asked suspiciously.

"They're the best ones."

"No, they're not."

"Then why can't I have any? Are they all gone?" I tried to peer into the clear plastic bag.

"I ate those first," she said.

"Well played," I credited her. Looking around to see if her grandmother was up yet, I was starting to think she would make a better conversationalist than the sassy girl. But then I just came right out and said, "You know, Zenobia, it's not easy being a zombie technician."

Her one eyebrow rose up a little. "You're a zombie technician?"

"Best one in town," I said importantly.

"The *only* one in town," she said, gazing dolefully out the large living room window at the gray morning, and brazenly popping a foldover into her mouth.

My eyes narrowed on that infernal bag of chips and then at her deceitful face. "Doesn't that make me the best?" I asked knowingly.

"All right," she sighed loudly, giving in. "How did you get to be a zombie technician?"

"First of all, it's zom tech, okay? I'm a zom tech 5," I explained patiently. "Second of all, it takes major skills, including unspeakable courage, unchecked rage, and serial nad-thumping ability. Next of all, it's not easy, okay? It's very demanding. Why do you think I'm grumpy all the time?"

"You're grumpy?" she scoffed in a high-pitched, disbelieving voice.

"Yeah, Z. My work is hard and it makes me grumpy."

"What about zombies do you 'tech'?" She was smiling now, munching on another foldover tortilla chip, and I could feel myself getting snarky.

"You wanna know something, Z? They say there's more than one way to skin a zombie. But I only know the one. That's how I'm wired. You wouldn't even know, okay? How could you even know?"

Not even trying to hide her giggling, she said, "Okay, I'm asking—how did you get to be a zombie technician? Did you go to school for it?"

"This is what you need to know: I'm the zombie fixer. I fix zombies."

"Fix, as in neuter?" she asked in a smart-assy way, trying to be funny.

"I've done that."

"Gross! You have not!"

"I solve solutions, Z. I make them go away."

"You mean 'problems,' and when did you ever make one go

away?" she snickered, and that was the camel that broke the straw.

"You know what, Zenobia Paccorelli? You never support me. I'm gone." And I stood up.

But the neck pain hit me like a stifling wave of my gross and sweaty Aunt Irene's foul pickle breath, and I stopped. Some of those zombie fighters are skilled, and the ones with octagon experience were the ones cheating the most, especially that one redheaded dude the size of a gorilla with hands like waffle irons. The worst part was that little piece of straw sticking out from the corner of his mouth—that made me go mad cow!

Reluctantly, I sat back down real slowly on her sofa, trying not to move my head around too much. It felt like my head connector was going to fall off, and I was starting to hope it would. I rubbed my neck hernia without looking at Zenobia, wondering how to put her in her place; she can be so contrascending sometimes. I stole a glance and noticed a glimmer of a smug smile crease her lips while she uncaringly munched away on two more foldover chips. Dammit, Z!

Shamelessly, she put the bag down on the floor behind the chair, probably so I couldn't get at it. Then she got up and sauntered over to the sofa, where she stood for a couple seconds before sitting down beside me.

"Hey, I know," she said, trying not to sound too excited. "I just learned this new massage technique. Let me try it on you." She was smiling like it was Christmas morning, and an icy chill shot through my chest. Maybe she *was* a succubus.

I could feel my heart gears grind as they shifted without warning. "I don't know—maybe you should try it on one of my zombie fighters."

"Shut your blower," she said and started reaching for my neck like Count Chocula.

"Is it gonna hurt?"

She didn't say anything.

"Is it going to hurt?" I repeated, a tad nervous and pulling back.

"No," she muttered softly, not altogether convincingly. Maybe it was because of the way she snickered like a hell-demon.

"Hey, you know what? Maybe you should try it on that cute zombie guy you like first," I ribbed her. I know how disgusted the zombies make her, so I couldn't help myself. Plus, I needed to stall until an idea hit me.

But there was no stopping her. "Yeah, some other time. Are you ready?" She sat straight up so that our eyes were almost at the same level.

"For what? Wait, why do I have to be ready?" Full-on fear was kicking in and my brain engine was pumping a mile an hour, trying desperately to devise the perfect getaway plan.

Like a determined predatory lioness in the Sahara, Zenobia crept around to the back of the well-worn sofa. "All right, let's get started," she hissed behind me, sounding like the proverbial grass in the snake. Her hands were on me then, rubbing the sides of my neck with firm, skillful strokes. After a couple minutes, she gently rolled my head around in big, lazy circles. The muscles really started loosening up!

"Hey, that's pretty good," I murmured, feeling the soreness disappear.

"That's just the beginning," she purred in her best breathy Marilyn Monroe, digging her hungry, deft fingers a little deeper into my neck beef. "Here comes the good part."

For a second, I dropped my defenses and was thankful to be sitting. I suddenly felt dizzy, and my knees trembled, like they always do when she talks like that. Then, just as quickly, Scotty threw the shields back up as it registered in my brain that there was danger in her voice; she was a little too enthusiastic.

Cautiously, I told her, "No, I don't want no good part. That feels pretty good, so you can stop now." I moved my neck around. "It's fine, thanks." I tried to slide away from her, to the edge of the sofa where it was safe, but right then her hungry hooks vised around my helpless neck.

"Just wait—the good part's coming up," she repeated stubbornly, like she hadn't heard me. Powerfully, she continued to slowly roll my head around like one of those gyrocopters getting warmed up.

Sensing danger, I panicked. "No, Zenobia. That's good—you're a miracle worker—thanks."

Now, I don't know why, but there's this thing about Zenobia. It can't be explained by scientists, but I can tell you that after you've been around her for, maybe four seconds, if you look into—and all the way through—her eyes, you know there's something going on way back inside there that demands respect, and fear. Even though at that moment I couldn't see her, I sensed it, and I got scared. She was clutching the back of my head and neck alarmingly tight, and I knew I should have been bolting.

"Don't get your girdle in a knot, grandma," she whispered throatily. "Get ready, now. Here comes the good part."

"No!" I started to pull away, but her betraying, torturous clamps were switched to maximum pressure, and they were imbedded so murderously deep into my neck fibers that escape was futile.

CRACK! Without warning, she jerked my head down so hard my left ear smashed brutally onto the top of my left shoulder, and I saw little white twinkling Christmas lights in a black tunnel, and it felt like a twelve-foot Viking sword had pierced the side of my damn neck.

"OW! Shit, Zenobia! What the—"

CRACK! She yanked my head down to the other side, and

the searing pain transported me into a wildly swirling black Slurpee machine, where I was spinning around dizzily, unable to see because I was legally blind from the eyes up.

"*¡Espera! ¡Santa Madre de Dios!*—Wait! Holy Mother of God!" I screamed as manly as I could, and she released her grip.

"Isn't that better?" She danced around to the front of the couch and grinned sinisterly while watching me with impish, evil contentment in her satanic eyes. I believe she really thought she had helped me—or hurt me, which I think are the same in her world.

"Do you know how bad that hurt?" I yelled angrily. "If I had two junkyard Dobermans chewing on my nuts right now it wouldn't hurt as bad—two, not three!"

"Why not three?" she asked with fake innocence, which I ignored.

"Cripes, Nurse Ratched! Do you listen?" I screamed at her furiously. I was so wasted from pain and the weakness that came with it, I let my broken body slide helplessly off the couch and onto the floor like the beaten-up doll of a homicidal first-grader with explosive anger disorder. Carefully, I clutched my busted neck with both hands to see if it was still there. As I lay on my face in the deep brown shag carpet I muttered, "*Estoy cerca de la muerte*—I am near death," but not loud enough for Satan's daughter to hear.

"I wish." She heard me. Standing over me with her hands on her hips, Z grumbled, "What a baby! You're welcome, momma's baby."

An unkind giggle bubbled from her before she gave me a withering look and nudged my shoulder with her foot, like you'd do to see if that snake in your grandmother's flowerbed would strike—and it did, didn't it, dumb-ass? What'd you think? It's a *snake!* Remember Dad on the porch swing, spewing beer from his nose and howling in delight while you screamed like that femmy kid in fifth-grade sex ed class and danced around the yard with that furious copperhead latched onto your motorcycle boot?

Now, as I slowly turned my swimming head to the side to look up at Zenobia, I glared at her with what I hoped looked like intimidating, enraged eyes. "For what? Why did you have to do that, after I told you not to? I think you knocked out a filling! Plus, I must be death cuz I can't hear a word."

"What word?" she asked.

"What do you mean, 'what word?' "

"You said you can't hear a word, *estúpido*." She was losing patience.

"Yeah, I can't see, either. You blinded me. Way to go—now I'm blind and I can't see. Thanks for not listening! Jeez, I'm probably paralyzed too. Quick, touch my arm! Can you feel anything?" Gingerly, I moved into a sitting position with my back resting against the couch and held out my left arm.

She knelt down and grabbed it, squeezing hard. "Can you feel that?"

"I don't know, can you?" I panicked.

"Yeah," she snorted.

"What does it feel like?" I asked loudly.

"Your arm, stupid."

"Good. That's a start; I'm finally on the road to recovery." I exhaled while looking down at her white fingers burrowing into my forearm. "Jeez, you don't have to throttle it!" When she didn't release right away I snatched her hand and pulled it off. "God, can you ever just listen once? Why don't you go ahead and give me some more 'good parts.' Jeez! Did you hear me when I said I didn't want any 'good parts'? Did you? Do you ever listen?"

"Can you see yet?" She was waving her stupid hand in front of my face. The polished ebony stone in her garish gold ring reflected the flickering, orangish candlelight, and behind that, I could see a mischievous grin forming on her black-painted lips. She was clearly having a lot of fun with the whole thing.

"See what?" I grumbled.

"Can you see anything?" Zenobia yelled in my ear.

I looked around the room quickly. "What are you talking about?"

"You said you were blind, remember?" she yelled even louder.

"Why are you yelling? I never said I couldn't hear," I shouted.

"Yes, you did!"

"God, can you just leave me alone now? Don't you think you did enough damage? Why don't you go hire yourself out to a mad scientist? He'd promote you to Igor on your first day."

"I bet your stupid neck doesn't hurt anymore." Her eyes danced and she was smiling impishly.

I glared at her. "No, the numbness is stopping the pain." And you know I was bitter. Then, feeling the need to get something good out of all this, I asked her, *"¿Tiene chocolate milk fría?*—Have you got any cold chocolate milk?"

"No."

"Yes, you do. Your grandma always makes sure she has some on hand for me. Frosted animal crackers, too."

"We're all out," she said without looking at me, which meant she wasn't in a sharing mood, which meant I must have said something recently to make her unsharing.

Delicately, I lifted myself up and onto the couch. I carefully turned my broken neck to study the ebony-haired angel of pain. She sat innocently on the edge of the rocking chair, leaning forward with her elbows on her knees and hands over her mouth to cover her snickering. Obsidian eyes pierced me and danced with . . . what? Evil? Joy? I couldn't tell.

"I wrote a song for you," I said after a stretch, still seething.

"You did?" She looked happy.

"I hope you like it. It's a special little song called 'Why Don't You Ever Listen?' "

"Suck it."

"I wrote another song for you. You wanna hear it?"

"I don't know, do I?"

"It's called 'I Don't Want the Good Part.' "

"You're such a baby."

"There's another song I wrote for you. It's called 'Your Grandma Says You're a Bad Girlfriend and I'm Not Making That Up.' "

"Stop writing songs for me!" she yelled toward my deaf ears.

And then, just like every other time, she fixed those demonic, coal-black eyes on me and ramped up the intensity. Ten seconds later, I wasn't mad anymore. It's magic—sometimes hurty magic. But she's really got me. It's weird, but when I look at her I see a precious doll . . . filled with sneaky evil. Maybe she cares too much, I don't know. I do know that her powers are unstoppable—like mine when I'm destroying backyard mutant zombie fighters, only different. But just as dangerous.

"What you don't seem to understand, Z," I said, skillfully changing topics, "is that when I was a kid, I had what I guess you would call a medical condition; I don't know why, but I loved to belch. One time on Easter morning when I was about eight or nine, I belched so violently I passed out and slipped into a coma. I woke up three days later and all the candy in my Easter basket was gone. Now, I don't want to blame anybody, but my dad had this suspicious look on him and he avoided me for a week."

"Your problem is you don't have any manners."

"Yes, I do. I got a couple," I said, thinking about it. "So, about how many would you say there are?"

"I don't—*what difference does that make?* Can't you just be nicer?"

"I can be nicer, yeah. I thought you wanted me to use manners."

"That's what I'm saying. You need to use manners when you're around other, normal, people. That way they don't get offended and hate you."

"Who hates me now? Is it Quinn? God, I hate that guy! I'm going over there right now. What did he say about me? I wanna know so I can throw it in his face as I'm beating him down." I was boiling.

"Quinn didn't say anything, Axel."

"So, he's keeping it in, huh? I'll get it out of him. I'll beat it out of him!"

"Quinn doesn't hate you. At least, I don't know if he does. Now shut up and listen; you're not hearing me right. I'm saying you need to start using manners before you end up really making someone mad."

"Manners? What does that have to do with Quinn? Wait a minute. I think I see. Quinn told you to threaten me with the manners thing, didn't he? Oh man, I hate that guy. I'm going over to his apartment. Where does he live? Is it in an apartment?" I headed for the door.

"Will you shut up and listen?" Zenobia bristled as she pulled me back by my shirt. "Jeez! I can't even remember the last time I saw Quinn McCloud. It's probably been about three years."

"Not Quinn McCloud. Quinn Humphries."

"Oh." She thought for a minute. "Yeah, he might hate you. I talked to him a couple weeks ago."

"I knew it! I'm gonna grind him up!"

"Okay, but about the manners: you *need* to start using good manners."

"Okay, sure. Right now, though, I'm gonna go work on Humphries." I bolted out the door, excited for revenge.

"Get . . . back . . . here," Z growled in that low, severe tone that meant I'd better listen. So I stopped and slowly turned around. She stood in the doorway, looking like a bull about to charge. I watched her for a second.

"Have you got a hearing problem?" she snarled.

"No."

"Do you want one?"

Reluctantly, I stepped up onto the porch and trudged back inside. A dangerous pause hung in the air, so I chose my words carefully.

"Z," I said calmly, releasing a big puff of air, "don't be jealous that they call me the zombie smiter." I had just cleverly distracted her again.

"Who does?" she huffed in that angry tone that shows me she cares.

"Everybody. Obviously it's cuz, you know, I smite zombies and fight zombies and keep the area safe and clear. I'm doing it for us, Z."

"Us? There's no *us!"* Her face turned scarlet, and if she'd been a cartoon, smoke would have poured out of her ears.

"At least until you finish college, Z. After all, you don't expect me to support us on just a zombie smiter's celery, do you?"

"Are you serious? You don't make any money fighting zombies!"

"Smiting zombies."

"You know, Axel," she said, taking a breath and composing herself, "when I get my psychology degree, you're going to be my first patient."

"Cool! How much does that pay?"

"You don't make any money being a patient, stupid. But I

could probably write a book about it and make a million dollars."

"I mean, I can do it for a while, Z—just to see if it pays out. But in the meantime, you should write that book you were telling me about."

"Oh my God," she muttered.

And we had a plan.

3
HOW SHOULD I KNOW?

Before long, word starts getting out in our quiet little town of Karbunkle, population 8,234, about our zombies. And Skeeter, the talkative two-armed scav who lives under the bridge and forages for popcorn in the theater dumpsters, tells me one day that some filmmaker guy from the university is making a movie about the time I went into battle and three dozen zombies got wrecked up. Two days later, I'm getting in my car to go to work when I see this important-looking blue and white van parked outside the cemetery.

Suddenly, I'm thinking, *hey, this must be the guy Skeeter Van Marvelous was telling me about.* So I sidle over there all confident and whatnot. A tall guy in a yellowish suit and perfect hair is talking seriously into a camera that a short pale dude is pointing at him. I can see they're busy, but I just interrupt.

"Hey, man," I blurt out, "I heard you were making a movie about me."

"About you?" the suit scoffs and looks me over a couple times. "That's crazy."

"I know," I say.

Before turning his attention back to the cameraman, he makes a sour face and grumbles, "You don't even know me, kid." Since he's being rude, I decide to take up more of his time.

"I know," I agree, standing and waiting.

He looks back at the camera and starts to say something, but then he sees me watching him and says irritably, "So think about what you're saying. How could that possibly be? I've never seen you before today." Motioning to his cameraman, they begin to resume what they were doing before I got there.

Shaking my head, I chuckle, "I don't know. It's weird, isn't it? A hungry Skeeter Van Marvelous told me that."

He abruptly turns back to me. "You know Skeeter?"

"Yeah. He said something about a movie. It was nothing I couldn't pry out of him with my half-eaten cheese sandwich."

"Skeeter told you?" Now he's interested. "Hey, are you Axelrod?"

"Yeah."

"All right!" He's looking at me like I'm Billy the Kid. "You're the guy I'm going to make a movie about!" he gushes, and now he's a little impressed as he steps forward and shakes my hand vigorously.

"Cool, man. A movie!" I exclaim, smiling like a fool. "Have you seen our zombies?"

He stops dead. His smile vanishes and his face loses all color. "Zombies? You have zombies?" he asks in amazement. Then he trembles and takes a nervous peek over his shoulder at the cemetery before quickly turning around so he no longer has his back to the headstones.

"Yeah," I boast.

His overly manicured eyebrows rise up to his hairline, and his little green eyes dart around anxiously. Suddenly, he's shifting around like a guy in a phone booth dodging a hornet. "Hey, good for you there," he utters hastily, reaching out and patting my shoulder awkwardly. "See ya around, kid."

Then they both jump in the van and peel out, leaving me in a Grade A dust cloud to enjoy and shake out of my hair. Watching them go, I'm thinking, *damn that lying Skeeter—I'm getting my sandwich back!*

Okay, forget that guy. I know there are a lot of questions about zombies that need answering because I got a couple emails on the subject. Most people are wondering if this is the end of the world and should they repent. If you're worried about repenting, you've got enough problems already, so I'm going to ignore those questions and get to the important ones. That way, you won't be confused. After all, this is about you and your fear of bed-wetting, right? Or zombies, or whatever—how should I know? I don't even know you.

Okay, here we go. The first question I got was, "Do the zombies only come out at night?"

Answer: No.

The next question was, "Are you single?"

Answer: Yes, sort of.

I mean, if Zenobia were serving food in hell, I'd go out today and do something very evil to make sure I got there. But she just sees me as a friend now, I think. And speaking of Zenobia, you should know that she's independent and always on your case, so don't ask me if it's okay to date her—you don't have the guts. Then again, maybe you should see for yourself. No, just forget it—it's too dangerous. Okay, I'll tell you what, if anybody wants to go out with her, I'm just going to encourage him. That way, he can learn from his first mistake, which was going out with her.

The next question was, "Dude, hook me up with some movie tickets."

Answer: Are you mental?

I don't work at the movie theater anymore, so I can't get anybody in free—and that includes zombies. Was this question from a zombie? Why the hell are zombies emailing me questions about free tickets? They have computers now? Besides, think about it—I only worked there for like, one day, because that was my day job three summers ago. Move on.

The fourth question was sent by some dude who wanted to know how many free pizzas I could connect him with.

Answer: Okay, here we go again—NO FREE PIZZAS! *God!*

I am not gonna get fired just because you wankers can't shell out eight bucks for a pizza. Start paying! You know, the zombies pay me—did you know that? Yeah, they pay. And if they don't—which they never do—I take 'em down and strip something off them they know I want, like a sweet vest. That's how I cut out the middleman.

Okay, hold on. Confession time: nobody actually emailed that last question to me, but I included it because the next time I get stiffed on a delivery I'm going to have a violent conniption. I mean it—I'm not holding back at all, no matter what your sad condition is, Grandma Roberta. I'm tired of your lies! I'm going to take you to the ground and pull the money out of your damn apron pocket—even if you are in a damn walker. Then when I'm done, I'm boosting your walker and putting wheels on it and taking it to the skate park. Who's going airborne off the half-pipe now?

And how do I even know if you're a real grandma? It could be a clever disguise. You always wear that apron but you never bake nothing; grandmas always bake stuff, so what about it? That's what I thought! Or, if I have to I'm gonna snag something else of yours worth the eight bones, like that sweet oxygen tank. And by the way, before you answer the door next time, *put on some damn pants!*

Final answer on the free pizza is four words: No way, Jose.

Yeah, I'm talking to you, Jose Johnson—don't order any more pizzas, you spelunker! Where does all your money go, man? Snap out of your video game coma and go back to work. Who does that, orders a thick-crust raisin pizza when they can't even pay for it? I can't remember the last time you paid me, so you know what? That's it, you just made my list cuz now I'm riled up, Jose! You've been warned.

The next question I got was a bit spiky because it came from Mrs. Lopez, who wanted to know when her taxes were going to be done.

Answer: Get back on your meds, Mrs. Lopez.

I know you're like, a thousand years old, and that's cool, but I'm not a 'countant and I already have a job. I could probably *deliver* some taxes to you because I'm pretty good at bringing shit to the right house, but I don't know how to . . . do your taxes or whatever, so stop trying to bully me. How about a zombie instead? You want a zombie? I could bring you one. I know your address and I'd be right on time, and it'd be nice and fresh and hot. But why don't you just ask your brother, Dempsey, to do your taxes? Didn't he get out of detox last week? Or is he dead? God, I hope so—that bastard never tipped me, so that's what he gets. Am I glad Dempsey is dead? Yes. Am I happy he's burning in hell? I guess. Did I have anything to do with it? You can't prove anything—and besides, I could ask you the same thing. You have twenty-four hours.

Next question. Oh God, not this one again. I can't believe I keep getting this question. Okay, this is from old man Beezer on Oak Street, who asked, "When are you going to pay for my window, Alex?"

Answer: Mr. Beezer, first of all, that ain't my name. And for the last time, let it go, old dude; I did not break your garage window in the blistering summer of 1995.

It was probably zombies. Did you even bother looking around for zombie sign? Huh? Do the detective work, dude. Also, think about it: cripes, in '95 I was like one year old. Do the math—didn't they have math back then? Take out your ruler and work out the figures on your sundial. How the hell can a one-year-old kid break a window that's five feet off the ground? What do you think, I was Nolan Ryan? And how did I know that you had real glass in there and not plexiglas?

Here's another thing: I didn't even live in your neighborhood then. Do you think that when I was a baby I woke up one day from my nappy, picked up the perfect throwing rock, and crawled a mile across town just to vandalize your garage in my diaper? How do you know if I even knew your address? Plus, it would've taken a couple days just to get there; how many naps would that require along the way? Not only that, but don't you think that by the time I got there, after all that crawling, my throwing arm would have been too wonky to chuck rocks at your window, which already had a crack in it anyway? And how did I get back home afterwards, huh? Take a cab? Wrong—my diaper didn't have pockets for cab fare, you old scrote!

Let it go, old man, or you're gonna find me at your doorstep with your next pizza, only it ain't going to be your usual pepperoni with extra cheese in that box. It's going to be something much worse, like a backhand with extra fist. You're gonna eat it all, too. And how about if I deliver something special over to your place one night to break out all your damn windows, like a few zombie ninjas? You want a house and garage with all the windows busted out and tarnishing the neighborhood by attracting homeless cats and vagabond zombie lowlives? If not, then *let it go!*

And, last but not first, this next question is from a guy who I promised not to give out his name and it's Dion Studster from over there by the Goodwill, and he asks, "Is the world coming to a hellish, flaming zombie end?"

Answer: Obviously.

Okay, that's all the emails I got. Oh, wait—last Friday, when I was getting new tires on my Mustang, I was starving to death, so I walked across the street and hiked through the drive-through of the See Food Grill. I didn't go inside because I hate that one bug-eyed dude with the Spiderman neck tattoo who works behind the counter and thinks he's funny and you just want to mash those fries into his greasy face.

Anyway, after I gave them my order and walked up to the window, there was this smelly bum sitting on the curb in the shade of the drive-through sign, and he sure was curious about the zombies. So, after I gave him a dollar I kicked him out of the way. Then I stood by the window, waiting for my fish sandwich (I'm retarded for those things) and fries with no salt, and that homeless dude, who was wearing about fourteen shirts and had two pairs of ratty-ass socks with holes in 'em on his hands that made his grimy fingers stick out and I could see torn-up newspapers coming out of his shoes, started asking me zombie questions. Some of them were pretty good, so I answered them because they were taking infinity to make my fish sandwich anyway. Here they are, as best as I remember:

How did they become zombies?

Yeah, that's the real question, isn't it? But really, how the hell should I know? If I knew the answer to that, I could have put myself through private investigator school by now.

Here's what I do know about that situation, though. One night they crawled up out of their dirt beds and I think I know why: they questioned my manhood. Or, maybe they're the nagging type, and after a few years of hanging around down in their holes, they got frustrated because they didn't have anyone to annoy anymore, so they decided to try out that zombie thing for themselves to see if it would play. So there's your answer.

Also, I have another theory. This one involves the new taco place on Main Street. Their burritos are the greatest of all time, even after you take out the black mustache hairs. And remember, the day Paco's Tacos opened was the same day we moved into the cemetery house, which was also the same day the zombies came out. So think about it: could greasy, hairy, savory burritos really be the cause of zombies? No. But they are.

How tall are they?

Stay focused.

What kind of zombies are they?

Well, we got zombies in all shapes and sizes and ages, man. For a sample, there's this one skinny zombie dude who's like, petrified; he's mostly just bones and rags. The strange thing is, he's always puffing on a pipe made out of a stick but it has no tobacco in it, and he wears a crumbly straw hat on his bald dome—yeah, he's gotta worry about sunburn now, right?

Other zombies are new, like that Terry guy who worked at the video store. He was that androgynous movie geek who'd seen every movie ever made, and he always criticized your choices, and I didn't know for sure what the hell he was—a dude or a chick. Well, one night when I was shutting off the sprinkler in the backyard, that pasty zombie he-she staggers up to me and gurgles, "Late fee. Late fee. Late fee." I barely know what he's saying cuz I'm ignoring him and his dirty teeth.

I don't owe no late fee, so I tell him to shut up and I run away. But does he listen? Nope, he stumbles after me like I'm gonna shell out two bucks to a transsexual zombie for a stupid movie about an elite squad of assault monkeys that was super fake. Jeez, does he even work there anymore? You know what? Just for that, I'm gonna return it at my lesion, which is *never!* It's not even that good—he should pay me a fee, that's what.

When do they come out and what do they do?

Okay, first of all, forget everything you've ever read about zombies in the movies. That stuff just ain't true, except the part about them being zombies, because that part is true. Mostly, they come out at night, probably because it's darker then and they don't want to be detected or embarrassed maybe, but some of the independent ones can be seen staggering around during the day. And they're homebodies, too; they don't go very far, normally just around the cemetery and our house. Usually at night they menace us and try to get inside the house, but what's the point? Who's going to invite a zombie to dinner? We don't even have enough chairs, so whatever.

Here's the deal on zombies: they just do whatever they want, which is mostly the same stuff they did before they died. Some of them are real nasty, and I know it's because they were angry pricks when they were alive, so you gotta watch those dudes.

Also, you know how some guys are farmers? Well, the farmer guys who died and are now zombies usually try to plant stuff in our yard, which is hard for them because they don't have any equipment. Nevertheless, we see them out there digging in the dirt with their skeleton hands and they're ridiculous. Those can be some of the most aggravating zombies because they're destroying the flowers and grass in our yard. And guess what? I'm the guy who has to fill in all those holes, so if they don't knock it off I'm gonna stuff each one of them down a hole and finish 'em with a cement chaser.

Other zombies, like the biker zombies, hang around in packs, wearing their decrepit leathers and acting tough by smoking and pushing around the zombie nerds. Now, where the hell does a zombie get cigarettes? Ask anybody, no one knows. Or do they? No, they don't. Or they're not telling.

As you can see, a lot of the zombies aren't dangerous, just annoying. However, a few them were probably watching a zombie movie when they died, or they were cannibals, because they're the assholes that'll try to eat you. But that rarely happens. I mean, even though they try hard, most of those dudes are poorly equipped for eating anybody.

Think about it: most of them are super old, weak, and flabby. Plus, a lot them don't even have teeth anymore. What do you think, they have zombie dentists who fit them with new dentures, perfect for biting human heads? Wrong.

They come at you snarling and slobbering, and if you let 'em get close enough, they try to get to your delicious inner brain by gumming through your skull. What usually happens though, is you stand there waiting patiently for them to feed, but they're so hopeless you wait for like, forever because all they can do is make annoying slurping sounds and gum up your hair until it's a sticky mess.

We also have a group of poser zombies. They're not really interested in taking chunks out of you, but when the nasty zombies are watching, they fake attack because they're trying to fit in and want to be noticed. Normally, I avoid them because it's embarrassing and I don't like feeding their egos.

The feeble zombies now, they're different; they try harder to bite you. They wander around wearing this spookily blissful expression, like they're overdosing on Valium, and there's no quit in them. I think it's because they're so feebed out they don't know what else to do. I guess those are the dudes who were mental when they died. Or maybe they died really hungry—hungry for human steaks. The main point is, you gotta keep your distance from those loopy corkers (when you're not pranking them), or you'll end up on the menu.

What do they do in the daytime? Where do they go?

Okay, I'm glad you asked that because I know the answer. I've done some investigating, and zombies are pretty easy to track. You ever track a zombie? It's not hard because they never look behind. Do you believe that? They never look behind! No kidding—one time I followed this zombie around for ten minutes, and he never knew I was back there with my staple gun, pinning a note to his grimy, shirtless back that said *CROSSDRESSER*. So that part was easy.

I spent all my money on prostitutes.

That's not a question.

How come no one else sees them?

The cemetery is located on the outskirts of town off a dirt road that leads basically to nowhere, and there aren't many houses out that way. Also, most of the townspeople aren't interested in dead guys or zombies for some reason. It's funny though, because they act all sad when a loved one dies, until they chunk 'em in the ground and forget about it and party on.

At the very least, you'd think a few of the really angry survivors would visit the rotten pricks who finally died—to wiz on their graves and call them names and stuff; you know, for payback. But I don't see much of that, either.

Even though a few people have seen the zombies, they act like they haven't. And for those who accept it, I guess they figure that it's fine as long as it's somebody else's problem, like taxes and your Uncle Marty. You know the old saying: "The only good zombie is the zombie in someone else's yard."

How long have they been zombies?
Ever since they died, I'm guessing.

How old are they?
Some of them must be a gadillion years old. I mean, we have a few cave dudes, so I guess that's before George Washington.

What's going to happen to them?
What are you asking me for? What do I look like, a predicting guy who predicts stuff? Take off some of those damn hats.

Do they rock?
Okay, do I even know what that means? What the hell does that mean? Stop asking stupid questions and put away that flask, rummy. Jeez. All right, my fish sandwich is here finally, so take that dollar I gave you and go buy a hamburger for yourself so I don't feel guilty, you flanker.

Are you queer for zombies, boy?
Look my fist in the eye and say that again, motherphucker!

When I heard that dog barking just now, I thought, *well, that's a sight for sore ears*.
You're starting to flake. Interview's over.

All right then, that was my Q & A period with some homeless bum who, even though it was seventy degrees out, was wearing four winter hats. He should have been happy with the dollar I gave him, but no, when I was paying the drive-through girl, that lousy fooker tried to jux my fish sandwich. So I put a boot between his eyes and sent him off to hobo dreamland. Then I took back my dollar. And one of his hats.

I'm glad he was there though, because his questions got me thinking, and now I know my Great-Uncle Ripsaw is a zombie. I mean, he has to be. He's a surly dude, and he hobbles around like a pirate with two peg legs. It seems he's always looking for buried fireworks and hidden treasure, and by treasure, I mean my loot, because he's constantly after it.

Also, whenever he comes out of the bathroom he acts real casual and pretends he's unaware of the wet stain completely covering the front of his khakis. Next time, I'm gonna ask him if he'd like to sop it up with a wiz sponge or a pee monkey.

I try not to look at it, but one time that dark stain was the size of Lake Michigan, and it caught me in its tractor beam and held me there against my will. I struggled to look away, but my disobedient eyes didn't listen and remained glued to his soggy crotch in wondering amazement. Good thing for me he was half lit, because he didn't notice and moseyed down the hall, looking for Dad and reeking of wiz. I fear that one of these days that wet patch will exert its mind control over me and force me to tell my secrets.

The thing about Uncle Ripsaw is that he was a cop for about a year before he got shot in the head. After that, he got a little punchy. Then he got cancer. Now he's just plain nutty. Plus, that head wound gave the poor guy a speech problem. Meaning, he'd say 'peech problem, cuz he can't pronounce that first *s* anymore. Strange thing is, he's not even aware of it, no matter that half the time nobody knows what he's trying to say and it seems pretty obvious that it aggravates the shit out of us.

I remember a few months back when he came to visit, and he brought with him his nasty little son, Sawdust. Quickly, I hid all my G.I. Joes. If I didn't, that homely little pre-vert would make them do queer stuff instead of fight.

We were in my room when Uncle Rip swaggered in, boozed up and bleary-eyed, and announced, "Heard about your zombie 'ituation, Axel. Lucky for you," he rasped as he leaned in close and suffocated me with Jim Beam vapors, "I'm the Zombie Whisperer. I can 'mell those 'ons a bitches from pi."

Cockily, he puffed out his fat chest, and his eyes gleamed as he gazed around coolly, waiting for one of us to challenge him.

"Pie?" I asked.

He pushed out his chest even farther. "No, *pi*. You know, 3.14 miles away. But that don't bother me none, cuz I 'peak to 'em in a 'pecial zombie language. You're lucky you called me." His oversized head was arrogantly bouncing around like it was on a Slinky.

"We called you?" I asked, puzzled.

He staggered a couple steps toward the window.

"What's your 20?" he suddenly boomed in a commanding voice, sounding like a cop again. He was standing tall and looking official.

I gawked at him, confused. "What? Do you mean my 10-20?"

"Your 20, what's your 20?"

"I'm standing right behind you."

"You 10-8? What's your 'tatus?" His head was tilted back, and he was acting all big league while sniffing like Barney Fife and gazing around at the walls, evidently unaware he was still in the same room.

I was confused. "My what?"

"Are you 10-8? You on duty? What's your 'tatus?"

"You mean 'status'?"

He was all business.

"What's your 'tatus?" he repeated without emotion while staring out the window. He never looked at me or Sawdust. His thumbs were tucked in his waistband, and his bushy eyebrows were raised self-importantly, making him look like one of those wannabe cowboy tough guys in an old western.

"Um, I'm good. So, 10-4, Starsky," I smirked.

"Don't be a 'mart-ass. I'll 'mack you into last week, go back and get you, 'mack you forward back to this time and make you apologize," he growled. Then, he relaxed and stumbled over toward us, his face beaming in a broad, mischievous smile. "Hey, you boys wanna 'ee a 'car? You don't know this, but 'Weet Lady Cancer took my rubies 'everal years back. I've 'till got the dangler, but check out how they cut me up."

Uncle Rip started taking down his pants, but that's when Ma stepped into the doorway. She pushed him against the wall and told him she'd throw his ass out if he took off his pants again just to show the devastation to his undercarriage. Grunting and frothing like a herniated ape with a vasectomy, he staggered drunkenly into the living room, muttering profanities and clutching the front of his unbuttoned pants in his fist.

Now that I think about it, I don't think he is a zombie—he's probably just an ape, like that agitated silverback I saw at the zoo in Nebraska that one time. He sure sounds like one when he pouts. God, he's like, fifty-three years old and he pouts. Plus, one time at the water park he took off his shirt, and his chest and back pelts were as thick as a teacher's excuses when the standardized testing results come back. When he tried going down the slide, his shaggy back sweater gripped the surface and stopped him about halfway down. It held him there until he sat up and crab-walked to the bottom.

Bonus Question (I just now thought it up): Can apes be zombies?

That's a good question—and it's fine by me as long as they don't pull out a shiv and shank someone. Plus, I'll tell ya this much: my Great-Uncle Skiz kept a loaded ape in the trunk of his Chevrolet for a reason. Think about that for a minute.

And there's something else too: can you trust a monkey?

Never! I did once and got burned. And, you know what? Now that I think about it, my Great-Uncle Skiz used to say, "If it's not one thing it's . . . that other thing, that . . . zombie thing."

So the message here is never trust an armed ape locked up in the back of a burned-out biker's '67 Chevy Impala with the driver's side door kicked in. Zombie or no zombie, that's a self-fulfilling prophecy right there. Especially for the zombies.

Second Bonus Question: Is it true there is one special person in the world for everybody?

Okay, that sounds like a nonzombie question, but just wait till you hear what I have to say about it. You know how some people say there *is* one person in the world meant for each of us? Well, there's a little more to it than that. I can tell you there are actually two, when you include each person's zombie that's meant for him or her.

Of course, by now that number may be lower, meaning there might be less than one zombie for each person because of all the zombies I've put down in the past year. But it could even be more, because I haven't worked the numbers lately and there is just an assload of zombies.

So remember, you have one love person out there waiting for you to find them so you can get married or whatnot, and there's one zombie looking for you. Once you get them both out of the way—especially that second one—you're in pretty good shape.

Now here's the problem. Let's say you meet your love person first. That's good. But what could happen is she brings *her* zombie with her, and the next thing you know, her zombie goes after you. Then, your zombie shows up, and now you've got three special people in your life. One of the problems with that is two of them are murderous zombies relentlessly chasing after you, which isn't really fair. And for doing that to you, your new love is a thoughtless doinker. And the Devil.

On the other hand, let's say you meet your zombie first. Well, if you can't handle him you're going to have to go into hiding, which means you'll never be able to meet your love person. And you'll die alone.

Either way, you're screwed. You should have had a better plan.

Okay, now everyone's up to speed on our past, present, and current zombie situation.

The next thing is, you wanna know how it impacts your social life, right? Well, first of all, I have to live with them—you don't, so no need to worry. But if I were you—which I'm not—and I had to live with zombies—which I do—I wouldn't be emailing me with your concerns, cuz I got my own zombie problems. Besides, it'd be stupid to email myself—even though I wouldn't read it anyway, so email away, I don't care.

The good news is, it seems the zombies limit themselves to hanging out only around my house. Like I said, I've never seen them leave our property. The bad news is, most of them are not in good enough shape to journey very far, which is why I'm starting up a conditioning program for the weaker ones.

So if you live with us—which you don't—you have to adapt to living with the walking dead—which I do. And if you don't live with us—which you better not be—you don't have to adapt, unless you like adapting; then go ahead, that's cool. Change can be good, unless you're our new mailman, who obviously doesn't like change.

Yesterday he dropped off the mail while I was in the yard hosing the maggots out of our garbage cans.

"Hey, man," he said, nervously handing me a pile of bills, "I heard you're having trouble with zombies? What's that about?"

I looked up at the storm clouds rolling in.

"I don't want to talk about it," I answered. "I can't get any sleep at night. Those foul dirt-hipsters make a freakin' racket all night long, pounding on my window and scraping on the house. I get up in the morning and I'm worn out—I feel like going to bed. That's not sleeping. That's waking. While other people are sleeping, I'm in bed waking."

"Zombies?" His voice trembled. "Like from the movies?"

"Listen, Pete, I don't want to talk about it." I motioned toward the cemetery. "They're not from the movies, they're from those graves over there. Every day they come out and prowl around like homeless crackheads looking for a fix."

"What have you done to try and get rid of them?"

"I don't want to talk about it." I scanned the sky, trying to determine if it was going to start raining. "So far, I've managed to prank them, beat them, and abuse them. Nothing works."

"What are you going to do?" he asked as his eyes kept darting over my shoulder to the headstones. A cold wind picked up, and Pete's twitching fingers fumbled fretfully with the top button on his blue mailman's coat.

"I don't want to talk about it," I said. "I've got a plan that's going to shake the zombie world, though. It involves plastic explosives and massive amounts of accelerants."

"Wow. That sounds like a plan."

"Yeah, I don't want to talk about it." I turned off the spigot and coiled up the hose. "It's a good plan, but I'm not going to use it—too many hazards. That's why I have this other plan."

"Good luck, man," he said quickly. "Hope it works out. Let me know if you need any help, all right?" And Pete left way faster than a guy should who had just offered his assistance.

"I told you, I don't want to talk about it," I yelled after him, and that was that.

Okay, now that I've answered everyone's questions, it's time to let out the clutch and share some chronicles.

4
HAVE WE MET?

This is how the whole zombie thing started.

Last year, Dad just up and bolted for a month. We think he went to Nebraska or someplace where he doesn't have warrants. Then when he came back, he had a beard and an attitude and told us to get out. But we didn't do it; I mean, who's going to move out of their own house? Problem was, Dad had been going through a tough stretch, and I don't blame him for wanting us gone, because I know how things can get messed up and you need some alone time, especially when it's not even your fault. Of course, we didn't think it was right that he blamed us, though. So, Ma didn't take him too seriously, and I was working so much I was hardly ever home and didn't even think about it.

About a week later, Deputy Bruce showed up, and he had a court odor to convict us from the house. Dammit, Juan!

But we still didn't leave.

Four days after that, dumpy Deputy Bruce came back and informed us we had two days, and I made fun of his mustache.

Ma wasn't too thrilled about getting kicked out, but she sure wasn't broken up over it, either. They'd been married for twenty-some years and their marriage had run the course. It was probably mostly because Dad owed everybody money and spent half his time in jail. There were still strong feelings between them, but like my gross and gluttonous Aunt Irene and chocolate pie, they probably shouldn't be in the same room too often. Later that day, after Bruce split, Ma got some payback as Dad was in the doorway trying to barter with the wiry little pizza guy, who was getting flustered.

"Hey, man," the pizza guy howled with a sudden look of recognition, "don't you already owe me money?" Glaring angrily at Dad, he pulled back the pizza and held it close like it was an autographed picture of Elvis.

Dad straightened a little taller and frowned. "No—who are you?" he blistered and reached for the pizza.

"I'm the guy who gave you two hundred bucks a couple weeks ago. You said you were in the circus and that you'd pay me back before you balled out of town. Guess what? I found out the circus wasn't even in town!" The tiny muscles around the corners of his eyes were twitching, and that little guy wanted a piece of Dad real bad.

"That's because we were sold out," Dad countered smoothly. "Besides, how do I know you're who you say you are? I can't trust you; you could be anyone—maybe even some opportunistic pizza delivery guy looking for a handout. Look, man, you should get a job and quit trying to scam honest people out of their hard-earned money." Dad was in top form.

The pizza dude's brow furrowed as if he were concentrating on a difficult problem. "Hey, I have a job. And I'm an honest guy." His anger was tempered some by his confusion and sudden peculiar desire to convince Dad of his virtues.

"Good for you, son," Dad beamed. "That's better. Doesn't it feel good to get that out?" He sounded like Pat Robertson and he winked at the kid. "Look, I gotta go now. You let me know if you have any more trouble. I'm glad I could be there for you; you can be proud. I feel good about things now."

Dad patted the kid on the shoulder and began gently coaxing the grease-soaked pizza box from his loosening grip. The hitmatized kid's eyes were blank. His tensed-up body then sagged and he released the pizza into Dad's care. Grinning approvingly, Dad stepped back and gave him a nod to indicate he'd done good and that the issue was resolved.

And that's about the time Ma Vesuvius blew up for some reason. Maybe she'd just had enough of Dad's manipulations, I don't know. But I was sitting next to her when, without a word she stood up, walked over to the stereo system, and viciously tore the monstrous cassette deck off the shelf, patch cords and all. Next thing you know, she looked like a vindictive Olympic shot-putter as she heaved the bulky head-seeker toward the doorway. The solid-state console was up and away, hurtling perniciously, with Dad on its radar. He was completely unaware as he phony-smiled at the perplexed pizza guy while holding the unpaid-for pizza in one hand and reaching for the doorknob with the other.

That outrageous cassette player was the size of a suitcase and as heavy as a full-grown six-month baby. When it struck Dad in the back of the head, I thought I saw sparks, and he grunted like a nut-slapped bull elephant. The force drove him violently into the doorframe face-first before he collapsed lifelessly to the threshold with a loud *thud!* He was sprawled out with his torso inside the doorway and his face on the porch.

After completing its mission, the remorseless cassette deck careened off the door, gouging out a nice fist-sized chunk of wood just above Dad's instantly unconscious head, and shot through the doorway toward the terrified pizza guy. Luckily for him, he was quick enough to jump back just in time. He gaped fearfully as it tumbled wildly down the steps, still in one piece. Good old 1970s' electronics. It finally skidded to a stop on the sidewalk, twelve feet past the bottom step.

The good thing is, as Dad went down he let go of the pizza, and that magical beef and pepperoni pie landed right side up on the floor, next to a passed-out dude with a head injury. Plus, you shoulda seen that pizza guy's expression—oh God! Ma and me erupted, hemorrhaging uncontrollable laughter. In the span of about one second, the kid's face went pitch white and his mouth dropped open as his bulging eyes ping-ponged from Dad to the cassette deck and back about nine times like Buckwheat from *The Little Rascals*. Then, and he never looked at us, he turbo-scuttled down the steps like a mouse with severe nad rash and completely split the scene.

Ma acted like nothing happened as she brought the pie over.

"Axel, why don't you say grace?"

"Sure, Ma. Dear Lord, thank you for this pizza . . . and thank you for the smiting power. And, yea, as I walk through the valley of the shadow of mine enemies and I smite them, I want to thank you for allowing me to smite—"

"Axel!"

"Also, I would like to thank you for this root beer, and although I ask a lot of you, smiting-wise, I would like to ask you if you could possibly—"

"Axel!"

"Amen."

"God! Can't you say one prayer without talking about ass kicking?!"

"Smiting."

"Shut it!"

Twenty minutes passed, and when Dad finally began to stir, Ma and me were still watching *The Munsters* on TV and finishing off the pizza—how can you even get enough pizza? I got news for you: you can't. Anyway, Dad was lying there moaning like a guy in the hospital after hernia surgery who moans a lot. Then he took about ten minutes to stagger to a standing position. He was a bobblehead now, his rubbery neck bouncing around in semicircles as he tried to focus and figure out where he was. Biting my bottom lip so I wouldn't laugh, I watched him for a minute before peeking over at Ma, who was ogling his stupid clown face and snickering.

When she caught my eye, we both busted a gut. I guess when Dad was out cold, we'd painted his face with pizza sauce and savory pepperonis. Being only semi-conscious now, he was unaware of the new look we'd given him. His eyes were half open, and he was on his feet, but he was as wobbly as a two-legged table and completely out of it, head trauma probably.

I thought he'd be mad at us for yanking on him with the makeover, but his eyes were vacant and he wore this dopey expression like his brain had left the station, so I knew we were safe. After a bit, he mumbled something like, "Pipcorndandy," and floundered out the door on crazy legs.

Unfortunately for a concussed guy, that first step was as tough as the Army's obstacle course. He failed, stumbling down the next seven steps before face-planting on the sidewalk with an *oomph!* Concussed again. He struggled to his feet and muttered something about licorice testicles before wandering off wearing one shoe while Ma and me laughed and ate pizza.

Later that night, I asked Ma about the incident. She grinned playfully and asked me if I'd seen the horror on the pizza guy's face when that stainless steel tape deck bounced off Dad's coconut before nearly taking out the kid's appendix. We both broke up again, and pretty soon my abs were aching so bad I had to curl up on the floor and think of things that suck so I would stop laughing, like my gross and extra-large Aunt Irene, who wears a ratty housedress the size of a tent.

A few minutes later, we were calm again and had a talk. Ma didn't rip on Dad or nothing. She just stated matter-of-factly, "Ax, what your dad lacks in discretion he makes up for in bad decisions." I thought about that for a minute before asking her about Dad's face and the pizza sauce makeup. I suggested that maybe that was why he decided to throw us out—because sometimes we hack on him a bit. She considered it, then shrugged and replied, "Hey, people who live in grass houses shouldn't throw stones."

"Or cassette decks," I added.

Ma studied me out of the corner of her eye and said, "That was probably over the top," then chuckled some more.

"Maybe," I winced a little, and thought for another minute. "Ma, when Dad came back last week, he was changed. And when you think about it, over the years it seems like he was never home, and you two have had troubles for like, forever. Why have you had so many troubles?" I was thinking about all the world-class shouting matches they'd had in the past.

She didn't say nothin' at first, just cast her eyes down, thinking. Then she lifted her head and said, "Axelrod, you're only nineteen. If you run from your troubles they'll chase you until you die."

I looked straight at her. "What about after?"

"After what?"

"After that."

"No troubles are too great to run from, Ax," she encouraged.

"Right on, Ma." I smiled and, feeling satisfied, turned my attention back to Herman Munster, who was learning how to be a ballroom dancer.

Dad didn't come home that night, but we didn't worry about it because he was probably in the ER or unconscious in somebody's yard. With the law on Dad's side, we knew we had to move out though, so Ma went out the next morning and found the perfect house just for the two of us. Fortune was smiling on us, because that broken-down little house was sitting right next to the town cemetery. Man, what a piece of luck: a rustic two-bedroom home with a scenic view of death.

At first, I wasn't too stoked about living there, but after a while, it got real bad. I'll tell you this much: you're not living unless your backyard is the resting place for a million stiffs. For the first couple weeks, I tried to push that thought out of my brain, and I was fine during the day, but sleeping at night was a journey. The dreams were a trip and a half. I'd hit the rack exhausted, and I'd lie there trying to concentrate on anything but dead guys. But it was hard, like the summer I worked construction, or that day I went without chocolate milk.

Usually, I'd start by running movies in my head about calm stuff like fishing, or fun things like that puppy I never got, and after a few minutes I'd drift away, feeling happy. Next thing you know, I'm being chased by some horrifying *thing* while floundering in a strange, foggy dreamworld like something from Jimi's "Purple Haze." Desperately, I try to escape, despite slogging in . . . *knee-deep black sand!* My legs are churning, but I can't pick up any speed and I know *it* is gonna get me. I don't know what *it* is because I never look back, but luckily, it never catches me. Thinking back on it, it was probably a swarm of dead guys, or one big deadzilla guy the size of a Chevy S-10.

Man, it sucked. It was like being held prisoner in your car at the drive-in, forced to watch a tripped-out version of a Vincent Rice horror movie every night, except it was inside your skull and you never knew if it was gonna end. It took a while to get used to, I can tell you. No wonder the name of the cemetery is

Grave Sights—I didn't think about it too much at first, but for a while there I saw weird shit all the time, and my eyes weren't even open.

Anyway, our shabby little house is kind of crappy cuz it's like, a hundred and thirty years old, the real estate guy said. No kidding; I don't know much about architecture, but it reminds me of early *Amityville Horror*. And yet, it's also sorta cool, because it has a kind of antique charm. The ancient floors are wooden and uneven and creaky. Heavy, solid oak doors in the bedrooms and bathroom should guarantee some privacy, but they don't close completely, so you'd better not be doing anything cringeworthy in there because that's when someone's walking in on you. Every wall is covered in paneling, just like my friend's old lake cottage we used to visit when we were kids. The only difference is our house isn't a cottage. But it does have a lake, sort of. A lake of dead guys.

I always wanted to live out in the sticks, so I like that about the house. Also, it's got an angry cellar of hell. How do I know that? Easy—when you open the miniature four-foot plywood door in the kitchen, the blackest of evil black nothingness rushes up the rotting wooden steps, bringing with it a nightmarish odor to punch you in the face. That's when you frantically whip the flimsy cardboard-thin door shut and your terrified fingers fumble desperately with the tiny hook before eventually slipping it into the little ring in the doorframe. Relieved, you exhale and think, *there, let's see Satan get in here now.*

But it figures that no sooner did I get it secured when Ma noticed the nearly concealed door and told me to take the Christmas decorations down there for the summer.

"Ah, I don't think that's a good idea, Ma," I told her, trying not to sound scared.

"Sure, it is," she said. "There's not that much and I'll bet there's plenty of room down there."

Thinking quickly, I went into full stall.

"Ack."

"What?"

"Bah."

"What did you say?"

"Hist."

"Are you shushing me?"

"Phfft."

"How would you like to make new noises out of a new hole?" she said calmly, dangerously.

"It's just," I struggled, "I don't think they want you to store stuff down there."

"Who doesn't?"

"The people who used to live here."

She gave me a strange look and said, "That's ridiculous."

"What if they have dead people buried down there?" I half-whispered, hoping it would shake her and she'd drop it.

"In the cellar? No, they're probably in coffins above ground. That way they can come up and get you easier." She was smiling.

I went over to the TV and said, "Hey, I know. Let's see if *The Munsters* marathon has started."

"That ain't till Saturday. Now go get the Christmas decorations."

"There's only one thing, Ma." I was really sweating, and this was my last chance, so I gave it everything I had. "It smells like somebody's been spanking werewolves down there and that's bad for my asthma."

She looked at me like I was covered in grasshoppers.

"Asthma? Really, Axel? You suddenly got asthma? Is that the best you could come up with?"

"All right then," I suggested apprehensively, "go ahead and take the stuff down there—I don't care. Doesn't bother me. I won't stand in your way. I got some other stuff to do anyway."

For an instant, she nearly went David Banner and Hulked out on me. Then, with folded arms and a look of exasperation, she leaned against the chipped, yellowed counter and let out a long, loud breath while regarding me thoughtfully.

"Axel, honey, your excuses are so weak only a dog can hear them."

Luckily, right then my phone rang. Silently thanking Jebus, and without looking at Ma, I wheeled out the front door to answer it. I didn't go back inside until after Ma had left for the store. Then I cleverly stored the Christmas stuff in the shed.

The thing to remember about Ma is she's got a load of raditude, which I think comes from her lethal, chopped-up blond hair, like that Samsonite guy in the Bible who had wicked-long hair and fought lions. If you're a smart cookie, you step lightly around Ma when there's any sign of conflict. Usually, I back down right away because I know her past and I'm not stupid.

Here's the thing: not many people know this, but long ago, in a dark, barren place where spectral images of the damned walk above ground seeking out those souls unfortunate enough to remain unclaimed, Ma wandered, and wondered. She was in deep thought as she contemplated her life's path. The red death moon rose and stalked the sky as it looked down and mocked those below . . . and waited. That's when Ma met the Devil at the crossroads. Brazenly, he stood in her way, and she punched him in the nuts. When she saw that he was the Devil, and realized what she had done, she kicked him in the nuts. She may be a little crispy around the edges, but she's fearless and hates being told what to do.

One time I saw her choke out a stray pit bull that was trying to bogart our supper pizza. The poor pizza guy had just stepped onto the porch and rang the doorbell when he saw the vicious beast coming from the next yard, so he dumped and split. The greedy canine ignored the kid and went for the pie—our pie! Ma was standing in the doorway about to hand the kid a twenty when the four-legged thief launched itself toward our supper, which was now tottering on the edge of the top step.

That arrogant boner never knew what hit him.

Ma was on him like whiskey on your grandma's breath on Christmas morning. A minute later, that mongrel was out cold beside our porch and Ma was carrying in the still-hot pizza. Thanks for coming, Fido! That hound got Handeled. That's Ma—you wouldn't know it unless you've seen it.

I don't know what the deal is with her hair though; something maybe, I don't know. As I said, I think that's where her power comes from. Weird, huh? She's always on me to do something with mine, but I'm just letting it go for now. Besides, my power doesn't come from my hair—it comes from my anger. And my large supply of beating power.

Speaking of hair, there was this one time I was in the chair at the salon when the girl looked at me kind of funny and said I assembled her brother. I didn't say anything because I'd never seen her brother, but I started thinking that maybe we were twins. Then when she started cutting my hair, I suddenly got this itch real deep in my ear. You know how, when you sit down and she wraps that cape around you, and your arms are pinned underneath, you feel like one of those crazy dudes tied up in a stray jacket in the asylum?

Once the girl does that, you're not allowed to move until she's done cutting. Of course, after you become her prisoner, and she starts pushing your head around and clipping off hair, that's about the time you get a little itch somewhere, like maybe in your ear. You can't do anything about it because you're afraid that if you move she'll cut a hunk off your head.

Well, that one time I got a real deep itch in my ear, and I

fought it for about two minutes. Finally, I couldn't take it anymore so I reached up and pushed my finger in for relief. Problem was, the itch was too deep. My finger was too fat and couldn't scratch that far in. It was too deep! Without moving my head, I glanced around on the counter for something I could jam in there.

That's when I realized the problem wasn't my ear itching at all. It was more like my outer brain was being tickled. I thought about that for a second and wondered how common *that* was. Since I didn't know how to scratch my brain, I decided the only thing I could do was think of something funny to get my mind off it, like my gross and gaseous Aunt Irene mistaking (I think) a can of cat food for tuna and spreading it on a sandwich and greedily gulping it down.

Later, when I got home, I remembered what that girl had said about her brother, so I asked Ma why I never had any brothers.

"We don't have any other kids, Ax."

"Yeah," was my reply, and I was left to draw my own confusions.

Anyway, the day we moved into the cemetery house everything was swell.

For about an hour.

After we got our gear put away, which didn't take long because we don't own that much, mostly speakers and clothes and towels and furniture, it was already pretty late. I was so tired I hit the couch to drain and watch *The Munsters*, especially Lily, who was looking exceptionally hot. Ma was stretched out and motionless in the recliner with her eyes closed. After a while, she yawned really loud, like a freight train when that guy excitedly blows the whistle like it's making all his dreams come true; isn't it lovely how he treats you to that 4000-decibel ear-splitter a hundred and forty-seven times as he rockets through the city in the middle of the night?

Ma rose slowly from the chair, clearing her throat and mumbling, "That's it for me, Ax. I'm all . . . what do you call it when you're tired?" Her hair was sticking straight up in the back and her eyes were slits.

"Sleepy?" I guessed.

"No, that's not it . . . *tired*—that's it. Yeah, I'm really tired." And she shuffled down the hall to bed. I watched her trundle away, then I focused on the TV and Herman playing baseball.

A short while later, I felt myself drifting off, and I was in heaven. Everything was perfect. It was a few minutes after midnight. I'm settled into a nice, big, comfy couch, and the room was dark but for the soft glow of the TV, and this chick had her arms around me. It was nice, real nice. Pretty soon, she was, you know, trying to nibble at my neck. She was all hands and hair and incisors and suddenly I was all, *"Have we met?!"*

I jumped to my feet and peered disbelievingly through the darkness at the strange, frail figure beside me on the couch.

Shaking my head to clear it, I rapidly tried to recall the events of the evening. First, we moved into the cemetery house. Second, I did some mowing. Third, we had pizza and root beer. Fourth, we watched TV. Fifth, surprise date. *What?!*

For starters, I'd never seen the girl before, so that was the main part of the surprise. Jeez, one minute you're alone on the sofa, and then, what the hell? Another problem was she didn't have that friendly look that made you want to sit beside her and snuggle up. I watched as she slowly lurched to the edge of the couch, and a long, wet hissing sound escaped from her twisted, drooling mouth before she started chirping like a goat choking on a tin can. Then she found another gear.

In an instant, she was reaching for me in a way that clearly said she wanted to get close—very close, but we weren't even going steady! Stepping back out of range, I blinked hard and waited to see what was gonna happen. Hastily, she rose up off the couch and lunged lustily toward me. Without thinking, I thunder-kicked her in the neck. The force drove her up and backward before she plummeted heavily to the floor. Keeping my distance, I stared down at the intruder lying on our cheap, ugly orange carpet. Sprawled out on her side, her thin arms and legs were akimbo, her stringy, brown hair hung down over her greenish face, and she wasn't moving.

Warily, I toed her ribs gently with my kicking boot. When she didn't respond, I said, "P.S., how the hell did you get in here?" At first, the slender heap of rags didn't move or make a sound. I thought I'd killed her. I stood there in a daze, trying again to make sense of it all.

Had I fallen asleep and this was a dream? Couldn't be, because if I was dreaming, what the hell was crumpled on the floor in front of the TV? Can dreams do that? No, it couldn't be a dream, because who dreams of a rail-thin girl with filthy, tattered clothes wrapped around glow-in-the-dark skin trying to make out with you? Why would you dream that? And what about the part of the dream where I had to kung fu that musty-smelling ragpicker across the room and was now looking down at it? Is that a common dream? Does it have some important meaning, like a fear of suddenly finding yourself at the front of your classroom not naked?

And what if the dream is real? *Then* what is the meaning of the dream?

Maybe I didn't know the answers to any of those questions, but I did know that the TV was turned up to about medium volume, and it was no match for the hellacious racket that erupted without warning on the rooftop of the old house; I thought Bigfoot was coming through the ceiling. Booming lightning strikes shook the walls, and a deafening downpour assaulted the ancient, rotting shingles above. Risking a quick glance out the window, I saw it was suddenly raising cats and dogs outside. Our quaint little cemetery house was being mercilessly hammered by the storm of the sentry.

As I looked down at the motionless pile of decay, I wondered for a second if it was a magical storm—the kind of magic that brings unwanted, aggressive, skinny chicks into your living room. If so, that's the kind of magic I don't like.

Listening to the monsoon raging outside, I kept my eyes locked on the underfed intruder on the floor, who was beginning to squirm around a little. Focusing on staying calm while blocking out thoughts of magical mayhem, I felt awake and alert, certain now that I was not dreaming. But really, to what lengths do people around here take to get a boyfriend, I pondered. Seemed pretty forward to me. She had been stealthy though, and I had to give her credit. I hadn't heard a thing; that untidy girl came in as quiet as a mousetrap.

Then I thought that maybe it wasn't the storm that's supernatural, maybe she was the one with the magic. I just hoped it was good magic, the kind that brings presents and cupcakes with one-inch-thick chocolate frosting.

Keeping one eye on her, I cautiously stretched out my arm and switched on the lamp at the end of the couch. The light didn't come on. I twisted the switch on and off about thirty times. No light. My only option was to try it thirty more times. Still no light. Then, I reached over the top of the lampshade and twisted the bulb, and yellowish light instantly burst across the room. For just a second, I was lost in an intense amber veil that overpowered the pale illumination from the television. What had been uncertain shadowy eeriness immediately became our sparsely decorated and cobwebbed living room again. Only, this living room came with a spiteful renegade.

Stirring on the floor near our beat-up TV stand was a most

unwelcome sight, one that I guess I'd hoped was a kind of funny mirage and would disappear as soon as the light came on. But it was a bad mirage and it was still there. When I checked it out—this time in well-lit conditions—it was way worse than before. I thought my eyes were deceasing me!

A sickly, mangy-haired stick-chick about my age in a long, dirty, gray nightgown swayed from side to side on her hands and knees like a busted-up dog. Then she sluggishly struggled to stand up on scabby, twig legs. Her emaciated, lime-green face was focused hungrily on me, and she was sorta snarling and gashing her crusty, brown teeth like that one big, toothy fish on that TV fishing show when they pulled it into the boat.

Only, she was glaring at me like I was the bait and she was that wicked-fat guy whose tackle box is jammed tight with powdered donuts—did you ever see that fishing guy who always sits in the boat and wears a white visor? He's got a big pumpkin gut, and man, that thing is huge! How does he keep that monster fed? Just donuts? He probably eats the bait, too. Bait made of donuts, I bet.

Anyway, examining that girl carefully from my safe position behind the recliner, I recognized her expression as one I'd seen before—but wait a minute, we'd only just met! What was her problem? We'd had merely the one date—which I'd only recently found out about—and it wasn't that great. On the other hand, aside from the kick to the gullet, it hadn't been all bad. So, why the attitude?

I leaned forward slightly and informed her, "I think you got the wrong house, sister."

As soon as I said that, a checkerboard of black and reddish open sores on her cheeks and forehead pulsed and oozed viscous maroon crème. She got all crazy-looking, like that big, bubble-eyed fish on that TV show that didn't get no donuts. Worse, she didn't even return my greeting. She just leered and began stalking me as if I had kicked her cat. I didn't even know she had a cat! In a flash, I bounced over to the other side of the room to stall for time until a good plan hit me.

Five minutes later, we'd circled the living room seventeen times and no plan had hit me.

Ten more minutes passed, and still no plan.

Keeping up a brisk pace around the room, I tried talking to her, but she just snarled and weird-eyed me while reaching for me like one of those old-time sleepwalkers on TV with stiff, outstretched arms. A few laps later, I got a brilliant idea. First, I lured her into the middle of the room. Then, BAM! I changed directions on her. Ha-ha! Now we were going the other way!

Only trouble now was, I'd worked up a pretty good thirst and desperately needed a slug of root beer. I wasn't about to turn my back on her long enough to snag a can out of the fridge, though. Right then I started wondering how long this weird shit was gonna last. It looked like the psycho bakeshop was open for business and wasn't about to close any time soon. Therefore, and since this looper was a chick, I had no choice.

I hollered for Ma.

Keeping a watchful eye on the lurker, I moved when she moved. She was like a ravenous, one-legged crocodile prowling the banks of the Nile, urgently and methodically taking the direct approach but somehow unable to make up any ground. Before long, we'd traveled around the living room eighty-four times, and Ma still hadn't arrived. Studying my opponent closely as she hobbled recklessly around the furniture, I could see she was as nimble as a crazy old dude in a truss who keeps falling out of his wheelchair because it's one of those cheap ones—the kind old dudes always fall out of.

It was really late now, and since I needed to get up early to start on the cemetery chores, severe aggravation was seeping in. Ordinarily, an intruder in the house means bone-breaking time, but I couldn't crank on this one anymore because she was a girl, sort of. Still, I try not to hit chicks. *If only Zenobia were here! That trespasser would pay a high price for her bad behavior!* The only thing I could do was hold out until Ma showed up.

The decrepit girl continued snuffling and shuffling after me, hopeful mayhem gripping her screwed-up face. By now, she had slowed to a deceptively sluggish pace, so I had to stop behind the couch and wait for her to get dangerously close before I could panic and shout for Ma again. God, what was she doing back there, changing her hair color?

A second later, Ma finally shambled into the living room, her Woody Woodpecker housecoat on backward and her puffy eyes nearly all the way closed. She's always like that when she gets woken up suddenly—all fuzzyheaded and goofy. It was easy to see she wasn't going to be much help until she fully booted up. Fine, I thought, my internal blood temperature rising. It was too late for apologies because at that point I couldn't wait any longer. Outside, our roof was still getting the shit beaten out of it, so I decided to take the storm's lead and roll into action—chick or no chick. Enough's enough.

Like that famous prize-winning jumping frog from Calculus County, I hopped over the couch and vigorously gripped that undernourished girl's leathery throat with both hands and throttled it like it was her rotten cat, which I hate. Next thing I knew, Ma was roaring at me as if I were at the other end of the Walmart parking lot.

"Axelrod!" Ma screamed. "What the hell are you doing? Don't choke that girl!" Semi-conscious and a little off balance, Ma stumbled over to us. "Mess the bitch up like this!"

I turned my head slightly to see Ma wind up and land a devastating haymaker into the moldy girl's right eye with a loud *thump!* The only problem was, Ma always swings hard, and after her fist blew through the girl's papier-mâché face bones, her follow-through clocked me solidly in the chin and staggered me. I lost my balance and toppled forward into the girl, and we both collapsed to the floor, with me on top of the bone pile.

Immediately, I spun off of Ma's grody punching bag, which had been clutching the front of my shirt and trying to bite my face. Without hesitating, I scampered to the corner and waited there, watching Ma and the girl. Breathing hard now, Ma squinted irritably at her opponent while flexing the knuckles on her haymaker hand. The nutjob in the corner with the mashed-in eye was wriggling around on the floor, making old man grunting sounds and trying to get up for Round 2.

That's about the time my brain went offline. I guess after everything that had happened up to that point, my overloaded CPU needed to power down for a bit. Maybe it was my tired mind refusing to make sense of it anymore. A dreamy feeling took hold of me and it felt like I was floating, disconnected from the crazy scene playing out in the living room. Looking at the crazy chick through a thick haze, a dozen questions lazily meandered through my mind: *Who is she? What is she? Who ate the last cinnamon graham cracker and left the empty box in the cupboard?*

But I didn't even care about the answers. Instead, I watched a little white spider scuttle out of the broken part of the girl's skull where Ma had punched in a hole. It quickly entered a nostril, and as it disappeared, I heard myself giggling.

The girl had just one eye now—one good eye and one big hole. And one runaway eight-legger. Good move, spider. Seek safety, little homeboy. Right about then I realized something kinda important: Ma had just jacked up that girl big time, and the girl wasn't crying . . . or bleeding . . . *or staying down!*

That snapped me out of it.

When I looked over at Ma, it was clear more destruction was forthcoming. Shaking with rage, she had noticeably burst into full consciousness. And she was wearing her angry face.

"Axel!" she shrieked furiously. "What the jack is this shit?"

She reached for a drink of my grape juice on the end table. Fearfully, I noticed the glass had left a wet ring, so I knew I had something else to worry about when this was over, because when she saw that, she'd blow for sure.

"I don't know, Ma," I stuttered. "I—"

"Wait—I don't think I want to know. Don't tell me," she interrupted before taking a long, noisy drink and replacing the betraying glass, never taking her eyes from the moaning girl.

"But—"

"No, Ax," she snapped, eyeing me steadily for a second. "I don't want to know. I don't ever want to know, so just keep it to yourself." Sighing loudly, she gazed around the room as if searching for more vagabonds. Her eyes then rested on the gurgling girl with the punched-in face who was clumsily attempting to get herself upright.

"Fine," I muttered agreeably.

"Okay, tell me," Ma demanded, looking freshly perturbed.

She looked away from me and marched dangerously across the room, where she pushed the girl to the floor and held her there with one fuzzy-slippered foot on her throat. Quickly, I told her everything: the girl and the kicking and the choking and the cat, and that's when I realized I might have been accidentally cheating on Zenobia—*oh, shizz!*

All the while, Ma stood there and listened while staring hatefully down at her prisoner, who was drooling and meekly thrashing around like she wanted to get home to feed her cat. But Ma wisely pretended she didn't know nothin' about no cat, and she wasn't letting that girl up.

Without warning, the girl suddenly became a crazed dog, which was about the time I figured out we weren't dealing with your average gatecrasher. No, there was something not quite right about that rude chick; no living girl could survive the punishment we had thrown at her and ask for seconds. Also, her delicate features contradicted her strength, which Ma and I learned right then was comparable to a revved-up alligator. Somehow, even with Ma's weight still on her throat, the girl twisted around and whacked Ma with a powerful kick to the temple, sending her sprawling to the floor. The persistent girl sluggishly staggered to her feet and shambled over to Ma in rickety slow motion.

Ma jumped up in fast motion.

"All is fair in love and warts, Zompira!" Ma bellowed ferociously and executed her next maneuver.

Next thing you know, the helpless intruder was getting choked out by a psychotic Ma, who had slipped behind her prey with lightning speed. The lethal hook was in deep, and Ma held it for several minutes. Strangely, however, the spaced invader didn't go limp. She never went limp!

Ma bore down. The girl's skinny arms and legs thrashed around and she never quit. Then, her body suddenly jerked spasmodically and slumped forward to the floor. It didn't look right, though. There was something . . . not . . . quite . . . right.

I looked from the girl to Ma, and watched silently for a couple long seconds as Ma stood there, staring down at her hands as she clutched . . . something. I blinked and saw—

Ma had choked the head right off!

I was ass-jaking cuz I don't ever remember seeing Ma choke off a head before!

A twisted, lunatic expression hung on the face of the head. And the teeth, all chipped and cracked like little bird Chiclets, chattered madly in some new, clicking sparrow language. Then, in the corner of the living room, a few feet from where I stood frozen, I watched as the crazy girl's slender, headless, wrecked-up body . . . *got up off the floor!*

Very deliberately, it shambled awkwardly around the room

like a zombie with its head cut off, flinging its twig arms about and knocking stuff over, including the grape juice onto the couch! Bad move, because Ma was dangerously wired now.

There wasn't any doubt anymore—that wasn't a normal two-piece chick in our house. I began hoping the whole thing would end soon so I could go to bed and pretend none of it ever happened. Plus, I needed to get some air because our visitor was quite generous with her precious, lung-clogging stench, which was now suffocating my breathing tubes.

With the eagerness of a principal reaching for the beloved paddling board, Ma firmly gripped the grungy, misshapen head in her throwing hand, reared back, and heaved that hideous melon at its teetering body. Her aim was good. She drilled it in the frickin' locker, and the body reeled backward and crashed flat onto its bony back as the disconnected coconut recoiled madly off the stomach and bounced to the floor.

The tangled, spiderwebby hair wound around the head as it caromed under the coffee table, ricocheted off the TV stand, and rolled to a tottering stop right in front of me. Its mushy, gray lips were pulled back, and the damn thing was scowling like a rat wearing a hot sauce G-string. It fixed me accusingly with its remaining eye, like I was the one who had started it!

Then, the withered body unsteadily raised itself up again. It appeared to be searching for something. First, it turned to the right and paused for a moment before swaying to the left, where it stopped, moronically facing the TV.

Now, how the hell can a headless body watch television? What a momo. Strange thing is, it stayed that way for a few seconds. I was dumbstruck, wondering why it wanted to watch *Scooby-Doo* at a time like this, when it was an episode I'd seen a thousand times already.

As I gawked like a goon, it pivoted and began aimlessly staggering around again, headless arms swinging crazily, sending the lamp sailing into the wall. Then it cleared a bunch of knickknacks, a couple pictures, and some other breakable shit off the bookcase with vigor.

Ma's eyes went wide with rage.

"Hey! Don't be a sore loser!" Ma roared, and I felt the temperature in the living room go up fifty degrees.

Party time!

Not wanting to be an accidental victim of Ma's wrath a second time, I quickstepped back behind the couch, where it was safe. There was no question in my mind that our nasty houseguest was about to get caught in the tiger's web. Sure enough, Ma shrieked and went whooshing across the living room like an obsessed cyclone. But as she closed in on the headless body and prepared to drop the hammer, she stepped on a porcelain penguin and lost her balance. Her momentum catapulted her forward unsteadily and, ducking her head and shoulder at the last instant, she managed to throw the most devastating rolling block in the history of the NFL.

The girl never saw it coming.

Ma crashed hard into the front of the two scrawny knees. Three or four booming cracks thundered sickeningly as the girl's spindly, white sticks folded up like a third-grade teacher with a difficult student. Bodies slammed into the bare wall and tumbled to the floor, with Ma somehow on the bottom. After a second or two, she slid partly out from under the battered, cadaverous body, and I noticed the girl's frail drumsticks were bent backward at the knee like ostrich legs. Headless or no, that girl wasn't gonna be walking no more, I thought.

As she tried to free herself, Ma was slowed by two desperate, bony hands firmly strangling her throat. Wrenching them off with a determined grunt, she shrieked savagely at Corpse Girl, "You should have let sleeping bags lie!"

Letting out a short and maniacal cackle, Ma shot up to her

feet, a little winded but looking better, almost refreshed.

And smiling wickedly.

Without hesitating, she reached down with both hands and fiercely snatched up the headless girl's body by the front of its rancid nightgown. With furious purpose, she violently dragged that abdominal living dead thing out of our living room and through the back door. Its arms were still thrashing about, as if searching for more knickknacks or the TV remote, but the busted-up legs weren't moving much, just twitching a little.

Right then I saw my chance and took it. Lining up that girl's disgusting head, I took one step and bent it like Beckham. When my foot connected to the center of the scowling face, it took off like a rocket! Narrowly missing Ma on the porch, it missiled through the doorway at hurricane speed into the rainy night, its snaggly hair trailing behind like the tail of a kite. As if on a mission, that soccer ball head cracked off the side of the big tree by the driveway before deflecting to the left. I watched in delirium as my game-winning attempt bounced two or three times before scooting between two smaller trees near the fence. GOOOOOOOOOAAAAAAALLLLLLLLLLLLLLL!!!!

After that, it rolled into some tall, wet weeds—the ones that were so high I didn't know if the lawnmower would cut them so I took the best approach and didn't try. Just then, a frolicsome raccoon boldly hopped onto that hideous dome as if it were made of French silk chocolate. I scampered to the doorway and stepped past Ma for a better look, and through the rain I saw that nocturnal hero grinning at me. I smiled and gave him a knowing nod before slipping back inside and closing the door.

Joining Ma on the couch, I took off my boot and pulled my foot up onto my lap so I could rub my sore kicking toe. We looked at each other for a few seconds, trying to hear each other's thoughts. Neither of us said anything for a while. Then

Ma started in, and for ten minutes I had to listen to her complain about those unmowed weeds. And the rude girl.

When she finally finished, I gazed hopefully at her. "Do you think it's dead?"

She began massaging the red knuckles on her punching fist and looked toward the closed door. "Gross is such an ugly word, Ax," Ma corrected. "I think it's dead, though. It sure was gross."

"No shit," I agreed.

The only unfinished business remaining was the big, purple juice stain on the couch—thank God Ma hadn't seen *that* yet—and all the broken shit scattered around the trashed living room. But it was late, so we left the mess for the next day.

And that's how our first day with the zombies ended.

Well, when I think about it, I guess it was just the one zombie. And a cat—a zombie's cat. But the cat wasn't there, so just a zombie. That tried to make it with me.

The next day I was delivering a large Chicago-style sausage and mushroom to my friend Drift at his apartment, and I told him about the incident. Of course, he didn't believe me and laughed so hard he threw up a little and pissed his pants.

"Oh man, Ax! Shut up! That never happened!" he howled deliriously and dropped onto his ratty-assed couch that looked like it must have spent the better part of the last few years outside in the woods. Plus, it didn't even have legs; it just squatted on the floor, looking like nobody loved it.

"You weren't there!" I said heatedly.

"Hey," he said, grasping for air and holding his stomach, "it's too bad it wasn't Halloween, because that would have made you the Headless Whore's Man!"

He fell over onto his side, laughing like a schizoid hyena as tears began to roll out of the corners of his scrunched-up eyes, which made me madder. I walked over and stood next to him, putting my fists on high alert and staring down with dangerous fury as I considered my next move.

When he opened his eyes and saw how close I was, he choked back his stupid laughing, and the room was suddenly quiet. I recognized the look of fear as he glanced up at me and then down to my hands. Slowly and subtly, as if I wouldn't notice, he inched away from me and tried forcing himself deep into the safety of the stained cushions while watching me.

"What are you looking at?" I said, glaring at him.

"Nothing . . . your fist, is it loaded?" he said, swallowing hard.

"What do you think?" I whispered harshly. "Wanna find out?"

"How?" His voice trembled.

"What do you mean, 'how?' "

"How do you find out if it's loaded?" he asked, wide-eyed.

"It's my fist. I should know, shouldn't I?"

"Is the safety on?"

"Wanna find out?"

"How?"

"All right, that's enough hows. You're gonna find out right now." I pocketed my keys and bent over him. "When it's over, let me know your thoughts on it. We're always happy to hear from our customers."

And that's when I monkey-punched him in the side of the head and snagged his Snoopy mug off the coffee table for my tip. That's what happens when you judge my mystery date.

5

PIZZA AND CHURCH DUDES

Okay, grasshoppers, it's time to move on to the intense topic of zombiology. If you're allergic or have an abnormal phobia of zombies, this is where you get off—and go get some help for your embarrassing affliction.

Now, when we suspected we might have zombies, I was troubled. Then scared. Then I chipped off to my room for a nap. But Ma and I had a long talk about it later on, and everything made sense after that. I still remember how it went.

"Ma, you know there's something unusual about this place, right?" I asked, hoping she would consider moving.

"Listen, Ax, no place is perfect," she grumbled. "What do you want, a mansion in Beverly Hills with your own skatepark where you can ride your skateboard whenever you want, any time of day or night, and you can put your speakers outside so you can rock and skate, and you can call the place The Rock and Skate and feature live bands like the Misfits while charging customers five bucks so you can score fat stacks every night?"

She looked at me like I was retarded. But I wasn't—I was stoked to the core.

"Yeah, that'd be cool!" I said. "When can we move there?" I felt dizzy.

"Move where?"

"To The Rock and Steak! I'm so fueled! It's the best place ever!"

She frowned. "Hey! I already threw away our moving box. I'm not going to go look for another one. This is our house now."

Undaunted, I skillfully shifted gears. "Hey, Ma, did you notice the address on this place?"

She looked at me suspiciously. "312? What of it?"

"Add the numbers."

"Six. So what?"

"Say it three times."

"Six six six—oh my God, Ax! You know what this means?!" She gripped my shoulders with shaking hands. "It can't be true—we forgot to mail in the change-of-address forms!" And with that, she chuckled and strolled away, leaving me to grind my teeth and silently count to ten.

Apparently, though, even after giving it her blessing, she was having some misgivings about the house as she inspected the construction. She carefully surveyed the walls and ceiling, no doubt wondering if she'd made the right call. I sensed an opportunity, so I followed her down the hallway.

"Yeah, but this place has ants, Ma." I bent down and squished a villainous brown sugar ant on the paint-splattered baseboard with my thumb.

"So what?"

"And zombies. What are we gonna do about that? Ants and zombies, Ma." Now, I know Ma's tough, but I really thought she'd reconsider after the throwdown with Zompira the night before and was a little surprised she wasn't weakening, not even a little.

She sighed and then perked up. "Hey, you know what? No big. I've lived with dead people before, haven't you?" She was watching me closely, scratching her blond head behind her ear, hoping I'd understand. "Well, haven't you?"

"I don't think so," I muttered, thinking hard and hoping my answer was no.

Ma looked amused. "Well, then, there ya go. Something new for you. How hard can it be?" She was as optimistic as I was that sweltering day last summer when I was sure I could down a gallon of root beer without spewing.

"Probably about as hard as the crust on that evil deep-dish pizza last night. What happened there? Did you order the ass-hard crust just for something new?" I griped cuz I was mad.

"Hey," Ma said, turning around to face me, "you brought it home."

She sounded just like she did that fateful day last summer when I gambled and lost, spewing a gallon of root beer all over the kitchen floor.

I was starting to feel picked on. "Whoa, hold on right there, Ma. I don't make 'em, I just deliver 'em."

"Yeah? How do I know that?" she looked at me just as distrustfully as she did that unpleasant day last summer when I promised to clean the used root beer off the kitchen floor.

"Well, for one, it was so cold last night my car windows were frosted over, and I had to do a lot of scraping before I boned out, that's how. But the real problem was that I couldn't find my scraper. So what's up with that? Know anything about a missing window scraper?" I answered in an accusing tone.

She eyed me suspiciously. "Did you get fired again? Is that why you were late getting home with the pizza?" God, she sounded just like she did that ominous day when somebody spewed root beer all over the kitchen floor and I got blamed for it.

I hate it when she changes the subject, so I changed it back again. "You don't want me crashing my Mustang, do ya? I had to scrape my windows with my driver's license. You know how hard *that* is?"

"You probably got fired again," Ma huffed, just like that one regrettable day last summer when I forgot to clean up the root beer and blamed the whole thing on one of my devilish amnesia episodes.

Glaring at her, I said, "What do you think, I just get fired all the time?"

Her eyebrows rose. "Don't you?"

"You don't understand the pizza industry, Ma. It's very complicated." I followed her gaze up to the water-stained, off-white ceiling, where she was staring with concern at two weird, quarter-sized punctures a couple inches apart, apparently the work of a house vampire, probably known as a hampire.

Nodding knowingly at the bite marks, she said in her matter-of-fact tone, "Prince Mmbobo fired you again, didn't he? Didn't he? I know he did, Ax Handel."

I gave her my Clark Griswold look of disbelief. "You know what? How could you know? You weren't there. Were you there? I didn't see you there. Not only that, but did you know ahead of time that my windows would frost up, so you boosted my scraper? How was I supposed to see out the windows? Was that part of your master plan?"

She stayed masterfully calm. "A mother knows these things. You had that 'fired' look only a mother can recognize, that's how." Her arms were folded and her nonchalant, knowing eyes were laughing at me.

"Okay, I see how it is," I said, unwilling to give in, but not wanting to go another round, either. "You know what? I got two words for you: *what . . . ever.*"

She winked at me. "Don't worry about it, chief. You may have lost your job, but it looks like you gained some zombies." Her lips formed a half-grin as she nodded slightly.

I held her gaze for a long moment, then softly murmured, "I got hired back again anyway," before slipping past her and scooting off to my bedroom, where I closed the door to get away from people accusing me of stuff.

A couple hours later, Ma calls me into her room. I walk in and she's standing there with a serious look on her face. Coolly, she tells me to sit down and pay attention because she's only going to tell me this once.

"We may have a problem here, Axy," she begins. "Living here, I mean. It seems that our neighbors are overly friendly, and vicious, and . . . dead. One has been in our house, and that usually means there are others blundering around and . . . whatnot. Remember those two seedy-looking characters by the garbage cans yesterday? Now," she says, looking me dead in the eye, "this is important: I want you to know that if I ever . . . turn into one of those *things* from the cemetery . . ." She stops and says, "I've got a gun in the closet." She's watching me closely.

I'm so surprised I almost fall over. "You have a gun?"

"Axel, listen to me. If I ever get like that—"

"A real gun?"

"No."

Puzzled, I watch her for a second before giving her the look that says I give up. Finally, I mumble, "Okay. Good talk, Ma," and start to leave.

Calmly, she looks at me and clears her throat loudly. "Axel, did you know there are tribes in Indonesia that, if your socks don't match, they go to war?"

"Because of mismatched socks?"

Ma shrugs. "How the hell should I know? They're always naked and living in a jungle, so put it together. I wouldn't put it past 'em. Shit, do what you wanna do, that's what I always say. Listen, not only that, but when their zombies get out of control and start smoking everybody's cigs, they zombie surf 'em."

Now I'm interested. "Zombies? Zombie surfing? Sounds cool. Can we do that? Wait, what is it?"

"Zombie surfing is where they take a tied-up zombie that everybody hates and hold him facedown in a clearing. Then they attach a ten-foot leather thong from his hair to the nads of an ox. At the whistle, they slap the ox's nads with an ice-cold bamboo cane, and it bolts away in pain and resentment, dragging the zombie behind him. As it runs, the leather strap continuously tightens around the ox's nuts, making him go fast—fast enough for decent surfing. The excited and vindictive natives take turns jumping onto the back of the shamed zombie and surf him as the maddened beast drags him past the cheering villagers.

"After a couple laps, the terrific stress on the ox's tortured plums throws him into angry-nad high gear. He sprints for his nads' life as he frantically tries to escape the pain. At that point, it becomes more challenging for the brave surfers because that ox is really tooling and the zombie is bouncing all over the place, making it a tough ride. That's why they offer a bonus."

"A bonus?"

"If you stay on long enough, the appreciative crowd hurls sweet delicacies at you as you pass by."

My mind is racing. "Sweet delicacies? Like chocolate-covered peanuts?"

Ma nods. "Pretty much, I'd say. Only it's chocolate grubs and roasted monkey wangs with a cinnamon-flavored dipping sauce."

"Hmm," I consider. "Ma, why are you telling me this? Are fun-loving Indonesian tribesmen the masterminds behind our ill-mannered zombie neighbors?" Seems likely.

"Probably," Ma says. "But there's something else you need to know." Opening the closet door, she reaches way back inside and pulls out what looks like a shotgun, but how would I know? About the only thing I can tell you about guns is that they're a lot like my Uncle Reggie: stuffed with danger and looking to maim someone.

"Now, look," she says in a serious tone. "After they put me in the ground, I want you to make sure I stay there, got it?" She looks like Annie Oakley the way she's cradling that gun as if it's her best friend. "I need you to do something for me."

I'm stunned. "Ma, you want me to—"

"That's right. Call your Uncle Reg—he'll know what to do."

My brain explodes. "Wait just a minute, Ma. You get a gun but I don't? When did you get that thing, anyway?"

She stares me down. "Here's what you need to know, Ax: I have a gun and you don't. But don't worry, I'll protect you—I'm your mom."

I'm a little jealous, but mostly panicky. "Hey, hold on. How is this going to work? Suppose the zombies come in through my bedroom window tonight. What am I supposed to do, tell them not to attack me cuz all I have is a cap pistol, which, by the way, is out of caps, so what's up with that? Do you think they have extra caps? Doubt it. 'Oh, and one more thing, zombie guy,' I'll say to him. 'Wait here while I go get Ma Barker. She's got a real gun she'll part your hair with.' What a dumb thing to say. Why would I even say that to a zombie?"

Ma sighs heavily. "What are you making such a big deal for? It's just a gun. Man, let it go already."

"Well, that's easy for you to say because you're heavily armed. Maybe I should have my own gun."

"Axel, we don't need any guns in this house. Guns are dangerous. Do you know how many people get killed each year by their own gun?" she asks irritably.

"Two?"

She glares at me. "It's way more than that, stupid. I don't need you screwing around with a gun and getting shot . . . or shooting someone—unless it's your cousin Little Dammit." It's clear Ma has thought about this and is dead set against hooking me up with a firearm.

I shrug, realizing that it's really no biggie.

"Yeah, I guess you're right," I agree. "I don't need a gun anyway when I got Axelpower."

"There you go. See? All you needed was confidence."

"Thanks, Ma," I grin, standing up.

"Glad to help out, son."

She smiles at me as I step into the hallway and head for a date with some warmed-up meat lover's pizza with crust of stone.

A few minutes later, the pizza's all gone but I'm still hungry, so I'm at the table chomping down cheese popcorn when a frenetic Dad barrels through the kitchen door like he's the T-bone in a pit bull kennel. How'd he find out where we live? Wild-eyed and wearing his fugitive face, he locks the door and frantically scurries over to the window to sneak a look out in the direction of the driveway for pursuers. I throw back another handful of corn and watch the show. It takes a minute before his hunted eyes even notice I'm in the room.

Over the years, this has become a routine part of our lives. I mean, Dad's the kind of guy who treats people like $1 scratch-off tickets, and let me tell you, there's only one instant winner in that deal. Then when they realize they got hosed, the chase is on. Dad's always been pretty talented at hiding out, however, so good luck catching up to him. It's probably his best skill, because even though he's always on the lam, he rarely gets caught.

It turns out that today he's over for lunch, at least that's what he says breathlessly as he wanders into the living room, taking in the new house. He looks pretty haggard; his hair is a mess under a big, red-stained bandage, and he hasn't shaved for days. Whatever. He's still breathing hard when he saunters back into the kitchen and mumbles something about wanting to borrow my Iron Maiden DVD, which is probably the real reason he came over. Suddenly, I need a plan because, just like always, if I fork it over, he'll borrow it for good, as in plunder. I decide to use basic misdirection to get him off task.

"You're never gonna believe this, Dad," I say, closely watching his expression, "but I think we got zombies."

Panting and leaning heavily against the fridge, he suddenly straightens up and his eyes get so big they look all white. "You-you might try some of that special sh-shampoo," he stammers. Shaken and moving away from me with a concerned look on his grubby face, he steps around to the opposite side of the table. "Is that like rabies?" he says in a nervous voice.

"Rabies?" I ask, confused.

"How the hell did you get rabies?" he scowls. "You were playing around with those dirty raccoons again, weren't you? I told you, man, those things carry diseases." Worriedly, he scurries into the living room, pulling the neck of his shirt up over his mouth and nose.

Oblivious to his fears, I get up and follow him, remembering something. "Hey, did you see that rabid raccoon on that exterminator show? He moved real slow like he was completely paralyzed, and he was out in the daytime acting weird. They said that's not normal."

Dad muffles through his shirt, "That's a bad disease, my

friend. Stay away from it." Then he steps back a little. "And stay away from me, hey. I don't need any more killer diseases."

"Yeah, but I think we got zombies, and I don't think they have rabies," I explain.

"Zombies? You mean like, sick, dead raccoons running around and shit?"

"I don't know. Hmm, I guess there could be raccoon zombies. I haven't seen any. You think it's possible?" Dad knows about a lot of stuff from when he used to be a teacher.

He grimaces. "I know one thing, if your zombies have rabies, they sure as shit got it from those grimy raccoons," he fumes, like he has some history with the 'coons.

Nodding slowly while considering it, I say, "Yeah, you're probably right. But what if the zombies gave the rabies to the raccoons?" I'm sitting on the arm of the couch, trying to unravel this mystery while pulling at a wicked hangnail. I should get the clippers.

"I never thought of that," Dad ponders. "But that's a biting infection. How many times have you seen a zombie bite a raccoon? And how could it, anyway? Have you ever tried to even catch a raccoon? Those things are fast, and tough. They can really fight—tore me up something terrible one time in my go-cart. Not only that, but how are you going to bite through that thick fur? Have you ever seen how thick that fur is? And it tastes oily. Plus, do you even have the right kind of teeth? Go ahead, let's see you to try to bite through a raccoon's fur; I'll wait here. It's like biting through a squirrel's fur, only thicker. More like a squirrel in a raccoon's fur coat."

"You ever bite a squirrel's fur?" I put to him.

His eyes flash at me. "Once," he mutters nervously then quickly looks away.

"What hap—"

"Shut up!" he blurts, hiding his eyes from me.

I shrug indifferently. "Well, I guess I could try to bite a squirrel. Do you think they have rabies?" Dad seems to be the expert on rabies. And some sort of squirrel fiend.

He nods slightly. "Probably the same as the raccoons, only not as much because they're smaller. And feistier." He pauses, and his eyes glass over for an instant, apparently recalling an unpleasant incident. "But their fur is thicker than it looks," he says, his voice trailing off.

"Hey, how about this?" I say. "What if you took off the squirrel's fur first, then bit him?"

"I guess I could shave a squirrel—I just got a new electric razor from the Goodwill," Dad says.

"What if he gets embarrassed and vengeful without his clothes?" I ask, concerned.

Dad pulls down the shade and holds back the edge with one finger while he stares unblinkingly out the window at nothing in particular, and I see his eyes are glazed over again.

In a small, nearly unrecognizable voice he says, "I know that feeling . . . your friends stop coming around, everybody makes a fuss, they call the cops . . ." His words trail off again and his baby browns go blank.

"Dad!" I yell to snap him out.

If I don't bring him out of it right away, I'll have to wait a while before I can get any information from him. Sometimes it takes half a day for him to return from one of his involuntary, hallucinatory trips. I can only imagine the hell it must be for him as he travels to places where he revisits his demons.

"What?" He blinks hard, looking dazed but back on track. "Yeah, a naked squirrel, you say. I guess we could put a sweater on him. Hmm . . . with no fur, I guess he'd look like a plucked chicken."

"Yeah, a two-legged chicken, you mean!" I add, laughing.

Dad doesn't laugh. "More like a crack-piping devil chicken

hell-bent on pecking out your damn eyes." He's staring into space.

I rip off the hangnail and it's a bleeder. Why didn't I use the clippers?

"You're right, Dad. I think I'll leave that crack squirrel to the raccoons." I wonder how a rumble between a raccoon and a squirrel would go down as I wrap my bleeding finger inside the front of my shirt and squeeze it tight. Damn those clippers! Then I think of something else important. "Do raccoons bite squirrels?"

"I would if it bit me first," Dad mutters, starting to drift again. "Even more so if I was naked . . ."

"Dad!" I yell again, stronger this time, and he jumps.

"Good point, Martillo," he says, louder than he needs to.

"Dad, what about this: suppose a rabid raccoon bit a rabid squirrel? Would that reverse the rabies process, curing the squirrel of rabies?"

He's shaking his head, as if recalling that previous shameful incident. "No. At the point the bite was made on the naked skin, the energy would be so great they'd both go back in time." Dad's eyes begin to gleam.

"To what year?"

Those sage headlights are blazing madly now. "Middle Ages, of course. Probably the year 1172. That seems right." He's talking fast, really locked in.

"Wow! Do you think those two would rule the world back then?"

"Obviously, because the boost in the squirrel's rabies power would turn him into a supermethed-out rodent. Ninjad-Up Nuclear Squirrel, they'd call him. NUNS for short. Three feet tall and looking for revenge. *NUNS, scourge of the Middle Ages!*" Dad is positively fixated.

"Revenge for what?"

"Exactly," Dad explains. "Think of it: squirreloraptor, ruler of the dinosaur kingdom!"

"No shit!" I shout enthusiastically. "Let's see thesaurus rex try to kick his ass now!"

"King of the Universe!" Dad yells louder than me. Then a dark, troubled expression quickly spreads over his face and he shifts gears again. "I ain't going back there to get my nuts eaten by a frustrated dinosaur squirrel," he mumbles fretfully and drops beside me on the couch, his gaze fixed downward on his trembling fingers. "They can leave me out—I ain't going, Martillo. I ain't going this time." He's clenching his teeth and wringing his sweaty hands.

This time? Damn, sometimes I don't even know my own father. But, I'm in full agreement with him on the time-traveling thing. "Second that—I'm staying right here in front of the TV!"

"I demand a refund!" Dad shouts vigorously, thrusting his fist toward the ceiling.

Ignoring that last part, I try to get him back in the corral. "Well, in order to prove our theory, I guess we have to get a gullible zombie to bite a naked raccoon."

"Good luck if you do." Dad blinks back into the world. "First, you've got to find a raccoon that's already been shaved, because you're not using my new razor—I just bought it. And do you think a naked raccoon is going to just stand there and let some buzz bomb sneak up on him? Right, and then he'll good-naturedly say, 'Sure, go ahead. You can see my fur's already gone, so just bite off a nice pork chop from my flank. Glad to help out and cheerio, my good man!' Are you serious? They're more closed-minded than that, I can tell you. Sharing is not on their list of important things."

"I guess you're right, Dad," I sigh, feeling discouraged. "But at least we finally know why we hate those bare raccoons." I check my finger and it's still bleeding. I hate those clippers!

"Damn right we do." Then his expression changes. "Hey, what was that other thing you wanted to know about? Zom . . . zebra . . . what was it again?" Dad's scrunching his face, trying to squeeze the word to the front of his brain.

"Oh yeah, I forgot to tell you," I say. "I think we got zombies. I mean, yesterday when we were unpacking, Ma and me saw a couple of baked, homeless dudes wandering around the yard. They sort of looked like they could be zombies, or ragpickers, or baked ragpickers. Later on, when I went outside to beat and interrogate them, they were gone. So I think they were zombies. I didn't think much of it until we got one inside the house last night."

Dad freezes. "Zombies? What do they want?" he says in a hushed voice, restless eyes dancing around the room.

I take a deep breath. "Well, I guess I don't really know. The one that was in here didn't say that much." I start thinking about Zompira and can't come up with a good answer.

"Huh." Dad has his fists to his temples, concentrating. "Hey, think about this," his voice is rising and he looks excited. "You know how every time somebody breaks into your house you think they want something?"

"Yeah, like burglars and thieves and stuff?" Seems obvious to me, but he's got this mad professor look going on now.

"Yeah, man. Those dudes just want to rip your ass off!" he blisters. "But think of this." He's smiling crazily and nearly whispering with the exhilaration of it all. "What if, these . . . zom . . . bee-zom . . . what is it again?"

"Zombies."

He shakes his head briskly. "No, that's not it. It was something like . . . zom-ray . . . raisins—razors—ray— something . . . rabies? Was it rabies?"

"No, that's the raccoons. These are zombies," I repeat while backing away because he's moved well into my personal space, nearly crowding me off my couch cushion.

He nods. "Okay, fair enough. Let's agree on 'zombies' for now. Now, what if, instead of wanting to boost your best stuff, they were trying to give you something? Huh? What about that?" Excitedly, he moves to the edge of the couch and clutches his hands together.

"You mean, like those church guys who always come around?"

"Why?" Dad asks, looking alarmed. "Do you think they have rabies?"

"Maybe." I hadn't thought of that. "Maybe that's where the zombies got it from, those church dudes." I'm thinking I'm on the right path.

Dad abruptly changes direction with a little spasm and a wry grin. "Maybe they got cool stereo equipment."

"Those church guys? Yeah, probably. I think they're rich."

"Probably." Dad thinks for a minute. "Hey, do you think they might give me a sweet subwoofer? I mean, mine's distorting like a chain-smoker with tuberculosis. You know what? We should migrate over to their church and check out their killer sound system. I'm in need of some new monster bass, so we should see what they've got."

I stand up. "I'll go get some CDs we can try out once we sneak in."

"Yeah." His eyes are dancing now. "Hey, did you ever find out what those zombies want to give you?"

"Not yet. What kind of stuff do zombies usually give away?" I wonder.

"Well, I don't know, specialty stuff like . . . birthday stuff. You know what? Maybe it's your birthday. Is it your birthday?"

I frown at him. "Dad, you don't know when my birthday is?"

He flinches, like he's hurt. "Hey, I'm not the zombie on trial here. But you know what? Maybe they like to celebrate too. What do you think? Do you suppose they're trying to give you birthday presents?"

My heart starts to race. "Maybe. But, do you think they have anything cool? Cuz that'd be sweet."

"Well, boy-o, we're just gonna hafta find out!" Dad pops up and enthusiastically claps me on the shoulder. He's grinning like it's Christmas morning and he's not in the joint. "Maybe they got something for your ma and me too, like a killer sub."

"I just hope it's not cheap crap that breaks down right away," I gripe, thinking about that junk.

Dad scowls and punches a fist into his palm. "Those bastards! They can just keep that crap. Why would you even give that away? Who does that? Sons a bitches! I hate those guys." He's pacing back and forth now. "Hey, do you think they have any gas barbecue grills? Because I need a new one."

That gives me an idea. "Do you think I could sell them your old one? I mean, it's a few years old, but it still works."

"Sure, why not. I don't like grilling and I'll never use it. How much do you think you could get for it?" He's very interested.

"Well, I don't know. Maybe we could swap it for something. How about a portable CD player?"

Dad looks pleased. "That's a pretty good idea. Okay, you make the deal, and I'll bring over the grill the next time I visit. Hey, just make sure it's a quality CD player, not the kind where the CD gets stuck in there and you have to listen to it over and over—unless it's a good one, like The Hives."

"Okay, I'll call you when the deal goes down. I hope they need a grill."

"Damn right they do." Dad stops and looks at me, and his expression softens. "You know what? This is just like that time you were watching *The Munsters* and you didn't understand what it was about, and you had to ask. Remember that?" Acting fatherly, he has that look he gets when he thinks about me as a youngster.

"Yeah, I forgot about that." I smile and punch him softly in the arm.

"Then there's your answer right there, nutlocker," Dad says proudly.

"Yeah, I think. But I forgot what that episode was about."

Dad's face goes blank. "What episode?"

"The one with the stuff, or something, you know."

"Listen, man," Dad says, suddenly perky, "if there's one thing I know, it's how to tune up a '72 Chevelle."

"You only know one thing?"

Confused, he mutters, ". . . no . . ." in a small, quiet voice, and now he's far away, thinking hard. Deep lines crease his forehead.

I watch him in silence for a second as I think about the sweet new CD player I'm about to get. Dad's deep into a daydream, probably thinking about bogarting the sweet new CD player I'm about to get.

Then he blinks and says, "Knock knock." And right away, I know he's trying to redeem himself.

I say, "Who's there?"

"My fist."

"Dad who?"

"What? I said knock knock," he says.

"Who's there?"

"My fist."

"Whose fist?"

"I'm gonna beat your ass," Dad scowls, getting worked up.

"Fist who?"

"What?"

"My fist," I say without looking at him so I don't laugh.

After a few seconds of silence, except for the sound of Dad breathing hard as he fights down the rage, his fury mysteriously slips away. That happens sometimes, and I don't know why, but usually it's a good thing. His shoulders sag and a wide, lazy smile crosses his face.

"Okay, stop," he says. "Let's get some breadsticks with the pizza this time. I'm starving."

"Breadsticks who?"

He doesn't even look at me. "Your ass and my boot."

I grin and say, "Nope, orange you glad I didn't say banana?"

He glares at me like I stole his *Jake Speed* videotape, so I quickly change the subject.

"Hey, Dad, Earl's Discount Coffins is having a blowout sale. Everything's marked down. Do you know anyone who needs a coffin? Now's the time to buy. He's got 'em all, and I'm not kidding. He's got plush jobs, cheapy cardboard ones, and everything in between."

"Now how in the hell would you know what kinds of coffins this guy has down there? What, have you been hanging out there on your days off?"

"Yes."

"What? What the hell for?"

"It's kinda cool in there. You should see his showroom; it's pretty interesting. Like I was saying, he's got infinity coffins on display. His high-end models are unbelievable."

"What could be so unbelievable about a coffin? It's a coffin. It's where you go to die."

"These are more than that. Some are like little luxury hotel suites for eternity. And they've got tons of wicked gadgets."

"Gadgets in a coffin? Like what?"

"Satellite TV with a big screen, for one. Also, they come with surround sound stereo systems and air conditioning."

"What?" He's pissed. "You're making that up, Axel. Why

would a damn stiff need that stuff? How the hell is he going to change the channel, huh? Can you answer that one?"

"They even got vibrating back-massaging pads, a tanning bed unit in the lid, and a wet bar."

"*What?* Now why in the hell would a corpse need a good tan? I'm not listening to this anymore. The goddamn dead guys are better off than I am, and they're dead! *Goddammit!*"

"Yeah, and that's not all. One of them has a hot tub and—"

"Oh God! Don't tell me anymore, I can't take it. Damn dead pricks—I could kill those assholes!"

"That's not all, either. One of 'em has a water bed with a vibrating pillow."

"Vibrating pillow?"

"And it has this thing that shows what the weather's like outside."

"That's enough, dammit!"

"Some of 'em have little swimming pools—"

"Shut—wait, really? Hey, last week I rode my bike down to the swimming pool."

"You did?"

"Yeah, to watch the kids swim. I thought of you, Ax, when you were a kid and how much you loved the water."

"Did you ever take me swimming? I don't remember."

"Nah, I never liked swimming, or taking you swimming, or watching you swim."

"Did Ma take me swimming then?"

"No, she didn't want to take you swimming, either. I guess you didn't like the water as much as you said you did."

"But last week you went and watched other kids swim?"

"Yeah, I watched for a little while and got myself a hot dog at the concession stand they have there. Put lots of ketchup on it, too. I ate that dog on the way home. Good dog. Yup, good dog that was."

"You ate a hot dog and rode your bike? Was it a footlong?"

"No, just my regular bike."

"Yeah, I like your bike, it's pretty cool, Dad."

"Not anymore. It's got ketchup on the handlebars."

And that was the day we finally solved the mystery of the rabid zombies.

6
PSYCHOLOGICAL TESTING

After Dad abruptly bolted out the back door a couple minutes later, I was left to think about the situation with the rabies and the CD player and whatnot. I thought that maybe, like Dad said, it was the raccoons that brought the sick zombies into our yard. But even if that was true, I didn't hate the raccoons. I guess it's cuz they don't know any better . . . or do they? Wait a minute—was this a clever trap? Now I really had something to consider. Just then, Ma came trudging into the living room with a basket of laundry, so I told her about it, and that we needed to start thinking about damage control.

"Ax, you're just going through a tough time right now." She dumped a load of towels on the couch and sat down beside it and began to fold.

"I don't know, maybe," I said, starting to miss my room in our old house and feeling resentful again about having to move into the new place.

She put a stack of clean white towels down on the coffee table and gave me a motherly look.

"You need to stop thinking about the cemetery and walking stiffs and stuff like that. What you need is to get away from here for a while and get your mind off it. Go see a movie, like a comedy. Or a horror flick—those are always good. A good zombie horror movie should fix you right up."

"You're right." I nodded thoughtfully. "Tonight I'm going to hide in the weeds and wait for the zombies to come out, and when they do I'm gonna rack their scraggy asses good. Then I'll be the one laughing at those raccoons. Who'll be the one laughing then? Me, that's what."

"See? Now don't you feel better?" Ma chirped.

"Yeah, good advice. Thanks, Ma," I replied gratefully and wandered away to call up Zenobia, because now I gots news for her.

I hit my bed and stretched out while punching in Z's digits. She's the smartest person I know, so I figured she'd have some good advice, or at least hide in the bushes with me. I couldn't wait to see if those wandering tards were actually zombies.

When she answered her phone I told her I had zombies.

She rudely told me I didn't get it from her and hung up.

I called her back and she was rude again so I hung up.

I called her again and she said I was mental and hung up.

I called her back and almost hung up, but then I apologized.

She was a little nicer and told me to stop over at her grandmother's house tomorrow after class, around four-thirty.

I told her to have chocolate milk and two boxes of animal crackers on hand this time.

She called me names and hung up.

The instant I knocked on her door the next day she eerily materialized on the other side of the screen, eating a grilled cheese sandwich. Straight black hair shrouded her face, as if attempting to conceal the evil intentions that lay behind eyes blacker than the depths of hell. The front of her T-shirt said *PLAY IT SAFE AND ASSUME I'M AN MMA FIGHTER.* She stood motionlessly—except for the chewing—in the doorway, staring at me intimidatingly for, oh, about an hour before mumbling for me to come in. That's her power thing.

Cautiously, I followed her inside and sat down. She smugly revealed she was going to give me one of those psychological tests to see if I was off balance. I gave her the okay, because I wanted to know, too—just as long as the test didn't reveal to the world any of my secret powers.

She rolled her eyes and, sighing loudly, told me she didn't need my permission, because she'd already decided to do it. Then she reached out and handed me half her sandwich, which was burnt on one side. She had cleverly tried to hide that part by keeping it on the bottom, but like a seasoned police defective, I knew it right off by taste. It made me choke a little, it was so nasty.

"Thanks for trying to poison me," I sputtered, accidentally coughing a piece in her direction. That foul chunk of soggy, black toast sailed toward her and stuck to the arm of her shirt, and she immediately swept it to the floor. Then, out of the blue, she flipped.

Steamrolling me with her eyes, she exploded, "Where's the poison? Because if you know where there's poison, I want some so I can give it to you!" And for a dark second, I thought I saw two-inch fangs gleaming inside that scarlet, devilish mouth.

But I held my ground. "It's the sandwich, man. Biting into that thing was the low point of my life." I flipped it over so she could see the scorched toast. "God, why don't I just lick the bottom of your black frying pan? Or is this one of those special sandwiches that comes with all the flavor removed? Jeez, you could use that thing to start a war. Or end one."

Then, while looking straight at her, I let my bottom jaw drop open, allowing that toxic gunk to tumble out and down the front of my shirt to the carpet.

For some reason she turned into a child of the damned, eyes shooting hellfire!

"Give it back, then!" she raged, reaching for the rest of it in my hand. God, she acted as if I'd wanted her half!

I held the sandwich at arm's length, up high and away from her. "You should ship this weapon of mass destruction over to Afghanistan. That'd help our boys out over there," I offered helpfully. Advantage: Axel!

"How would you like to die right now?" she roared, one fist gripping the front of my shirt and trying to pull me down, while her other hand stretched frantically upward for the unpleasant sandwich I held above my head.

"By eating more of that shit? Don't make me do it—it might make me queer for older chicks."

That did it.

"Okay, you know what? Shut up!" Those last two words she screamed loud enough for deaf people to hear as she released my T-shirt and stomped over to the rocking chair, where she plunked down furiously and glared at me with murderous eyes.

Bringing the repulsive menace down for closer examination, I studied it for a few seconds before pouring it on. "Well done, Z. This bastard's so vile, you could torture al-Qaeda prisoners by putting it in the same room with them so that they have to breathe in its vapors."

"You don't have to eat it, smart-ass!"

"Too late, I already ate some. Shit, now I can't see!" I tilted my head back and waved my arms wildly in front of me and staggered around. "Someone, please help me. Is anyone there?

Aunt Edna, is that you? Nod once for yes, and say 'no' for no."

"You're one in a million, Axelrod!"

"You mean there's a hundred more just like me?"

"Nice math," Zenobia criticized, starting to cool off a little and needing to get back on the rails. "Do you wanna take this test or what, toolbox?"

"Yeah, let's do it," I grinned and straightened up, glad this wasn't going to be one of those 'four days of mad at me' events. I still had to dispose of the rest of the offensive sandwich though, so when she wasn't watching, I stuffed that scorched bad boy in between the couch cushions as I sat down. Let the couch choke on that sombitch.

"All right then, jerkwad. Shut up and let's get started," she commanded irritably. Then she grabbed an open magazine off the end table and studied the page showing a quiz.

"You shut up," I muttered under my breath.

"What?" she barked, squinting hard at me. "Are you whispering in front of my back?"

"What?" I said, acting surprised.

She pierced me real hard with those accusing, steely-black hellhound eyes, and for an instant, I felt them stab my brain. I thought I was about to get ninja-ed, so I quickly looked away and lowered my head while concentrating real hard as I fiddled with the seam of my jeans, pretending like I had some very important business to take care of there. Using all my inner power, I kept my mouth shut and didn't make any sudden movements. The trick worked cuz she didn't attack.

After about a minute of malevolent breathing at me, Z cleared her throat noisily. Risking an upward glance, I saw her frown and look down at her magazine for a moment. Then she took a deep breath and jumped into the quiz savagely. It was over in like, four seconds.

She asked, "When I say 'yellow' what do you see?"

"Banana."

"Wrong. When I say 'donut' what do you hear?"

"Chocolate."

"Wrong. When I say 'cemetery' what do you do?"

"Prepare for danger."

"Wrong. You clearly have psychological problems, Ax."

"I know."

"Wrong. You're a bad boyfriend too," she carped.

I looked down. "Sorry."

"Wrong." She heaved the magazine onto the couch next to me and stood up, glaring at me. "I have to go now," she hissed.

I smiled a cautious smile and offered apologetically, "The fringe is looking good today."

"Thanks," she mumbled, self-consciously touching her bangs.

"Tengo sed—I'm thirsty," I said meekly.

"Shut up."

"I'm so hungry I could eat a bear," I said hopefully.

"You mean you're as hungry *as* a bear."

"A bare what?"

"What do you mean, 'a bear what?' A bear. Just a bear."

"A bare bear? How hungry is a bare bear?" I asked her.

"How would I know? Maybe he was hibernating all summer and all his hair fell out and he forgot to eat, that's what."

"Jeez, Z, now you're an expert on bears? Maybe you should write a book. Or come up with a cure for bear baldness. How many bald bears do you know, anyway?"

"Three."

"Three? That's impossible," I told her. "You're in school all day, and it's not bear school. Unless, hey, do they come through the drive-through at night at the Hamburger Pants? But they wouldn't be bald, now would they?"

"Why can't bears be bald? Is that a benefit reserved only for men? How is that fair? If we're going to share this planet with the animals, we have to treat them fairly. That means whatever we have, they should have too."

"Does that include dangerous girlfriends?" I said real low so she couldn't hear.

She shot me a dangerous glance that said she'd heard me.

"Now I've got a headache," she mumbled.

"Should bears have headaches too, then?"

"They already have enough headaches—everybody hates them and tries to shoot them. Or feeds their garbage to them. You ever eat garbage?"

"It's awful," I murmured, not loud enough for her to hear.

"You ate garbage?!" She heard me.

"No," I said. "Once."

"Okay, I don't want to do this anymore, Axel. There's really something wrong with you and I'm gonna go now cuz it might be catchy." She suddenly looked tired, or worn out.

"That's right. You go now, back to your comfy world with no hunger or baldness and no eating from the dumpsters. You like it that way, don't you?"

"Yes."

"You make me sick."

"Good. I'm leaving."

Then, reaching down and snagging a loop on her backpack, the brooding Zenobia hoisted it effortlessly off the floor and stomped out the front door, muttering, "Jackmonkey."

That left just me, sitting in her grandmother's house on her grandmother's couch like a tool, thirsty and starving. And her grandmother wasn't even home. More importantly, I had just failed a critical psychological evaluation, the results of which held all the answers I'd been looking for, and they just walked out the door.

I flipped on the TV to see if *The Three Stooges* were on, but it was turned to a religious channel and they were showing a church service. One thing they should change about church is, even though you claim it wasn't you, I think you should just expect that collection plate guy to hold that money dish in front of you for a longer period of time until you give the right amount. Because any time you have ongoing gas during church, you should have to pay extra for the trouble you caused by smoking out the people in the two pews behind you the entire hour.

After a minute or so, I turned off the TV and decided I was sane enough to at least go to work. Besides, those tasty pizzas weren't gonna deliver themselves, and sitting there wasn't getting me any closer to chocolate milk, or chow. And anyhow, if any insanity did happen to spill over, it would fall onto the customers, and that's their own damn problem.

7
GRAMMAR SCHOOL PAYBACK

This chapter is awesome. It talks about a zombie, how to neutralize a zombie, and how ridiculous zombies can be. But it doesn't say anything about zombie nightclub singers, because you know how outrageous that sounds.

Because I had a lot to do the day after I failed that important psychological test, I stumbled out of bed earlier than usual. I was still pretty sleepy and decided some outside air might help wake me up. When I took two steps past the back porch and tripped over a writhing, headless body, I damn near had an angiogram! My confused mind began racing, and for a second I didn't understand what was going on. Then I remembered the wicked rumble with Zompira a couple nights earlier. Since I hadn't used the back door lately, it's no wonder I hadn't seen her, and for some reason I simply forgot she was out there. Guess Ma did too, cuz she hadn't said anything about it.

That's when my memory powered up and I halted for a

second, replaying the details of that night. When it was over, I wasn't totally convinced that any of it had actually happened at all—it was just too crazy to believe. I thought that it must have been a movie I'd seen, or maybe even a dream. Then when I looked down, I thought, *some dream—the assholes don't even have heads!*

My plan for the day had been to take out the cemetery lawnmower from the shed and fire that mother up so I could get some more grass cut. Problem was, I didn't like the idea of mowing around a twisting, headless carcass. It had to go. But I sure wasn't in the mood to touch that foul thing again. It seemed the only thing I could do was watch it squirm for a couple minutes before kicking it good in the ribs, which made it spasm and lurch over on its side, where it twitched like a sunfish on the dock at Lake Asscrack (it's really Lake Asmond, but nobody calls it that).

Son of a bitch was a zombie, all right. What else could it be? Didn't even have a damn head. Without thinking about it anymore, I ducked back inside the house, where I bumped into Ma just inside the kitchen door.

"I couldn't mow the lawn," I told her, panting for effect. "The mower has a flat tire." I tried to look disappointed.

"What? How could that happen?" Ma asked, spreading grape jelly on a couple of toasts.

I thought for a second. "I don't know, I guess I ran over a nail or something."

"Aren't those lawnmower tires made of solid rubber?"

"Ours are plastic."

"Then how could you get a flat tire?"

"Oh yeah." My brain spun and searched for the perfect alibi. "You know what? I think what happened was I ran out of time. That must be why I'm not mowing the lawn."

She stopped scraping the inside of the empty jelly jar. "So, can you fix the tire, or do we need to buy a new one?"

"Well, I don't know where you can buy a tire for a lawnmower . . . Craigslist, maybe."

She frowned. "Can't you just put more air in it?"

"No, it's solid plastic."

"Then how did it get flat?"

"I don't think it is flat."

"Well, that's good news." Looking relieved, Ma took her plate of jelly toast into the living room.

"Yeah, that's great news. So you can go ahead and mow now," I murmured.

She looked displeased. "Ax, I gotta go to work. Can you have it done before you have to go to the Krust?"

"It doesn't seem likely."

"Okay, Axelrod, why won't you do it?" She knew something was up.

Haltingly, I mumbled, "Mainly because of the zombie situation."

"Is that all?"

She stuffed half a slice in her mouth and smirked in my direction.

I was staring out the kitchen window at the jerking body, mentally willing it to get up and stumble off. "No, I have other reasons."

"Are they better than that one?"

"Possibly."

"What are they?"

"Well, they include 'I'm not feeling it' and 'I don't see me doing it for some reason.' "

Ma frowned. "Ax, I know you ain't no baby." She shoved in another slice and stood up, facing me. "What about me? I got a toothache on my arm where that she-devil bit me the other night." Pulling up her sleeve to show me, I was horrified to see a blotch the size and color of a plum on her left biceps completely surrounded by teeth marks!

I screamed, "Oh no! For real? You're going to turn into a zombie!"

Sneering, she said, "God, I hope so. Then I won't have to work at that friggin' store with those damn idiots no more. Now, can you make it happ'n, cap'n?" She grinned and squeezed my arm. "Can you make the grass shorter?"

"Yeah, I'm on it," I muttered, thinking it couldn't be that bad, and rolled to the door, wondering why Ma wasn't concerned about entering the realm of the walking dead.

"Thanks, babe. You're my favorite son." I watched as she smiled and stuffed in the last slice of toast. "P.S., turning into a zombie after you've been bit, not gonna happen—that's just movie folklore," she scoffed.

"You sure?" I asked dubiously.

She was smiling confidently. "Woulda happened by now, right?" She socked me in the arm and stepped out the door to her car.

"Right on, Ma."

I bounced out right behind her, feeling happy I wasn't going to have a zombie mom, and ashamed that I'd almost chickened out of taking care of the headless punk in the yard.

A couple days before, I'd found out from Ma that because we live in the cemetery house we're also the undertakers of the cemetery. So instead of paying rent, we're responsible for taking care of the grounds and stuff, which is sweet because now I get to work outside, where I'm on my own and don't have to deal with stupid-asses telling me what to do. Plus, we've got a shed full of wicked tools I can use any time I want to build shit and wreck shit.

Once I was back outside, I had a better attitude and went to the shed to find a shovel to bury that zombie girl. For the grave, I chose a bare spot at the edge of the cemetery near the fence. When I started, it was really hard cuz you hafta dig a lot and stuff. Soon enough, I was working like the digging-est dog, and it wasn't long before I had a nice, cozy grave dug.

It took courage, but I went over to that herky-jerky body and scooped it up with the shovel and loaded it into a wheelbarrow. She was a bit gunky around the neck area, but I stayed away from that part. You should have seen the legs. They were gnarly bent and wrecked up good! Sick.

That's the first time I ever piloted a wheelbarrow, and it was kind of fun, except it had a dead body in it that was alive. The challenging part was tooling across the lawn at high speed while trying to prevent that darn cadaver from crawling over the side. Each time it was about to escape, I skillfully tilted the wheelbarrow in the opposite direction to tip it back in. But what an ingrate. Why would it want out when it was getting a killer fast ride? Did it have somewhere to go? Like, to meet with other headless corpses for coffee? Are you kidding me? That could never happen.

Once I reached the grave, I tossed the restless carcass unceremoniously into the two-foot-deep hole. Of course, it didn't like being in there, but too bad. Problem was, I felt I should put all the pieces in there together, but I couldn't locate that soccer ball head. Searching through the weeds by the fence produced nothing. Those clever raccoons!

Since it appeared I had no choice, I started to wonder how necessary it was to bury the head along with the body anyway. At first, I was worried that the two might be segregated for infinity years, and her lonely spirit body would end up wandering around blindly, bumping into stuff and looking foolish while trying hard to fit in with the other ghosts. And what about her ghost head? Would it bob around in the air like a lost balloon? Or worse, will it have to crawl around on the ground, being pulled along by its teeth and lips while avoiding fire ants and spilled ice-cream cones and fresh dog dook? Then I thought maybe a ghost doesn't need to have a whole body since it's a ghost. But maybe it does. Unable to really figure it out, I decided I was going to have to shake down those crafty raccoons and make them pay for their vile misdeed.

For the time being, though, I decided to fill in the hole and tamp it down good, because I couldn't have that girl climbing out of there and scuttling around the yard making a nuisance of herself. Truth is, I didn't know what else to do—it's not like there's a manual for that kind of shit. And if there is, who wrote it? Is it that one guy who's an expert on death and dying? Can I trust him? I wasn't about to take any chances.

Twenty minutes later, as I was patting down the last of the dirt on the grave, a strange sensation suddenly came over me. It felt like someone—or some . . . *raccoon*—was watching me. I glanced around for furry spies in black masks. After a couple of tense moments, I grudgingly put the shovel in the wheelbarrow and slowly drove it back to the shed, scanning the area the whole time. Once, I thought I heard suspicious laughter in the weeds, but I didn't see anything.

"Your day will come, Mr. Raccoon, bringer of mischief," I hissed under my breath. But now was not the time.

I stepped into the shade of the musty-smelling shed. The push mower still had gas in it from the failed weed-cutting effort, but I was going to be mowing acres today and wanted to ride. Grabbing the edge of the filthy, green tarp covering the riding mower, I yanked it hard and watched a cloud of dust rise as dozens of dead June bugs and yesterday's empty cream soda pop cans tumbled to the dirt floor. It was the first time I'd ever really had a chance to scope out a riding lawnmower, so I looked it over closely. There were only a couple thousand spiderwebs on it, and it looked like it might be fun to drive.

Then, suddenly remembering an earlier conversation about tires, I crouched down and saw that the mower had knobby rubber tires, and they were partly flat. After clearing the air compressor of several million more spiderwebs, I inflated all four tires and filled the gas tank. Then I fired that mother up and let it run for a minute. Eagerly, I jumped into the cockpit and examined the controls. They didn't look too complicated, so I rammed her into gear and roared out into the sunlight, clipping the doorway just hard enough to take out the bottom half of the doorjamb, but I didn't even feel bad about that. I had a date with the foot-high grass, and it was him or me. When it was all over, just one of us would remain standing.

"There can be only one!" I yelled heartily as I attacked without mercy.

Six hours later, I was sunburned and dying of thirst, but all the grass was cut. I left the mower by the shed to cool down while I plodded into the house. Standing in front of the fridge and cooling off while fishing around for a frosty, refreshing root beer, I was surprised when Ma came home early and wanted to know where the pancakes were.

Excitedly, I looked around and didn't see any pancakes anywhere. So, I was forced to confess that I didn't know where the pancakes were, but how could that be my fault, since this was the first I'd heard anything about pancakes.

"All right, then," she groaned irritably and hung her keys on the little hook by the door and sighed. "Axel, you're gonna need to start making pancakes for Saturday supper."

"What? Why?"

"Because."

I panicked. "Because? How is that even an answer? And today's Thursday, Ma."

"Well, that kind of thinking isn't going to get us any pancakes, now is it?" She folded her arms and frowned at me.

"So I have to make pancakes for *la cena* on Saturdays?" I asked, uncertain.

"Sounds good, doesn't it?" she said enthusiastically.

Sulking a little, I said, "I guess, but it seems like I have to be the one making the pancakes. And why for supper?"

"That's the rule, Ax." She hung her jacket on the wooden coatrack in the corner and winked at me.

"Rule? What rule?"

"The pancake rule. Hey, I don't like it either. But I don't make the rules, honey."

I stared at her in disbelief. "Yes, you do—you just made that rule."

She shrugged and said, "Well, somebody has to make the rules. What do you think, rules just make themselves, like pancakes? That's a stupid thought. How the hell is a pancake going to make itself? Could it even grip the spatula? And it wouldn't even know when it's done cooking—what if it burns itself? Do you even think this stuff out, Axelwood?"

"I just thought—"

"See what happens?" she interrupted, looking at me like I had no brain. "That's why we have rules in the first place—so we don't have to eat burnt pancakes. I don't want burnt pancakes. Do you want burnt pancakes? I could make you some right now, and it's not even Saturday. Is that what you want? It sounds like that's what you want. I'll do it. I'll make 'em and they'll be nasty-burnt. Is that what you want? How many do you want?"

"None. It's just that, I don't know how to make pancakes."

She looked amused. "Would you rather have *you* make the rules?"

My mood brightened. "Yeah, I would. I could make a lot better rules," I boasted.

"Name one rule you would make."

My mind raced. "Well, I might have this rule about no putting jelly on pancakes."

"Why?"

"Doctors say you should never put jelly on pancakes."

"Why not?"

"Because it tastes yucky."

Ma wasn't amused. "I don't know if we should allow you to be the rule maker, Ax. It seems like you have a lot of rules and stuff. I'll tell you this right now: I don't need to be strapped in by a whole set of rules. I'm more of a free spirit." She spread her arms out, pretending to fly.

"Sorry."

"It's all right. Next time don't say the thoughts you are thinking. Say something else instead."

"How do I do that?"

"Start by not even thinking those first thoughts. Instead, think other thoughts."

"Okay, I'll try."

As it turned out, Ma ordered a deep-dish pizza, and forty minutes later, we were sitting in front of the TV eating a large beef and mushroom pie and watching *The Addams Family*.

Halfway into it, Ma suddenly whispered, "Did you hear that?"

I froze. "Hear what?" I turned down the volume on the TV and listened intently.

"Footprints," she whispered, softer this time. Her eyes darted to the bay window behind the couch.

Quietly, I got up and crept to the window. Pushing the drapes aside a couple inches, I peered apprehensively into the early darkness. At first, I saw nothing. Then, as my night-vision eyes adjusted, I spied a shadowy figure in the backyard. I squinted to get a better look. *WTF?* Yup, there was a hobo out there all right, and that got me aggravated. He was sorta wandering around like he might be lost, but that's no excuse.

"Ma," I said coldly, "what do you call it when you see queer things that are actually there?" I didn't even care if the hobo heard me.

"Hallucinations?"

"No, it's that strange feeling that what I'm seeing is real."

"Ghosts?"

"Wait. Do they have hobo ghosts? Because, if so, then yeah, we got one out there right now. Plus, there's a herd by the cemetery gate."

"What? Come on, Ax." Ma wasn't impressed. "Are you trying to tell me you see ghosts hanging out way over by the cemetery?"

"Yeah, they're out there."

She was doubtful. "I don't see how, that's pretty far. How far can you see?"

"I can see the stars. How far is that?"

Sighing heavily, Ma got up and trudged over to where I was holding back the drapes.

"What the *dos?!*" she howled as she peeked out the window beside me.

It wasn't too dark to see a few dozen lamewads shambling about, nearly a hundred feet away. Some of them were teetering as they stumbled around in crooked lines and circles, and occasionally one would list a little too far and fall over. It looked like they were covered in dried muck and ooze and . . . icky stuff. Not only that, but a bunch of them were missing essential body parts, like arms and feet and common sense.

A lot of the women wore what must have been elegant gowns at one time, and the men were mostly in suits, or what was left of them. Generally, their clothes were tattered, and a few wore nothing but shredded rags. Some were even naked!

Oh man, the naked ones—God, I wish they hadn't been naked for me to see! I wouldn't wish that on anyone. You should have seen them! Discolored, rotting, naked zombie corpses. Instantly, my only thought was to unsee it, so I started for the bathroom to wash my eyes out with soap.

"We got a zombie situation, son," Ma rasped just then. I looked at her, and she said in a very serious tone, "Hey, Axy."

"What?" I whispered tentatively.

"You have a grave look on your face."

"How does that even help?" I said irritably as she snickered and pinched my cheek, but I was silently grateful that she'd distracted me enough to save me from a painful eye washing.

I peeked out the window and started to wonder if that guy from the exterminator show on the History Channel had a trick or two for removing this type of pest. Only, wait a minute—I suddenly recognized the lone trespasser in the yard who I had thought was a ghost hobo. It was Mr. Applebaum, my old fifth-grade math teacher who died about ten years ago in a boating accident and got killed. I never liked him because he was mean and piled on the homework, especially on Fridays. So now, because of that, he was *haunting* me? I should be haunting him.

The first thing I wanted to know was why did he want me to think he was a hobo? That was Mystery Number One. Mystery Number Two was how could I get some quick, quality extermination tips? I could check out that fishing show, because that portly fishing guy is pretty good at getting rid of fish out of the lake and donuts out of the box. On the other hand, I doubted if he had any good zombie experience, mainly because of his huge gut—you ever seen that dude's boiler? That monster has its own website. Maybe the exterminator guy had some better tips, since he's always removing unwanted raccoons, cockroaches, and girlfriends. I'd have to look into it.

Watching those goons by the fence, I began thinking that things were starting to get out of hand around here, and since I really didn't have time for fishing, maybe that raccoon exterminator guy was the one with the answer. Then again, maybe we could round up all those undead infiltrators and put them on the boat with that fishing guy. That way, he could dispose of them out in the deep water where the giant predatory fish prowl. They've got huge, sharp teeth that bite stuff like other fish . . . and maybe corpse guys from our yard.

Suddenly, I was struck with horror as Mr. Applebaum staggered toward my swing. My blood pressure gauge immediately rose a hundred degrees. He was nearly there, and that just wasn't gonna work. Zombie or no zombie, it was head-breaking time! My greatest strength is my strongest weakness, which is anger. Plus pure strength. They were both redlining as I spun away from the window and ran to my room to find Nine.

You see, one dark night many, many years ago, Dad was lurking in the shadows, chopping down the neighbor's elm tree. He claimed it was because he was tired of raking the leaves that fell into his yard. Only thing was, after a few strokes, the ax head flew off and sailed through the windshield of the guy's station wagon. Dad immediately hauled ass, and although he wasn't able to finish chopping down the tree, he stole the guy's gas grill.

Afterward, he felt bad about that, until he sold it to buy a new ax to chop down the guy's shrubs that bordered our yard in the back. Guess what? The very next week I was born. That got Dad thinking about how the ax head came off on the ninth stroke, I was born nine days later, and the exact time of the windshield incident had been—that's right—midnight. Dad took it as a sign. He placed the hickory ax handle in my crib, complete with a black 9 burned into it, and Nine has been with me ever since. The weird part is, for the first four or five years, Dad called me Nine, while Ma called me Ax. Somehow, Ax won out, and the hickory ended up being Nine.

Reaching under my bed now, I grabbed Nine, and after flicking off a reddish-brown spider, I slapped the handle into my palm, relishing the feel of its destructive power. Gripping it tightly, I ran out the back door screaming like a fourth-grader off his ADD meds.

Mr. Applebaum had his generously fat back to me as he stumbled ponderously closer to the rope swing I had hung up the day before. It's a really thick rope with a giant knot at the bottom for standing on, not intended for commercial use or overweight zombies. I halted twenty feet behind him in the middle of the yard. Not sure what to do, I waited uncertainly in the moonlight for his next move.

As he closed in on my new swing, I felt my face get hot. When he stopped before it and fumbled at the rope, I was afraid he was planning on settling his massive girth on it. Even though I'd used heavy-duty, thick-as-your-arm rope, the real problem was I didn't remember him asking me for permission, and common courtesy is important. I guess that's when I flew into a homicidal rage.

"Oh, no you don't!" I yelled and charged him.

Slowly, deliberately, as if he were waiting in line at the Dairy Queen, he turned around to face me. He gawked for a second with empty eyes, like a freshman reading a chemistry textbook. Then something clicked in his nearly vacant head and he rumbled toward me like a prehysterical tyrannosaurus hex.

With no lips on his fleshy face, he appeared to be grinning at me, and I don't like to be mocked. Also, when he got closer, my offended nose sensed that he hadn't changed his damn adult diaper in years, which is when I got mad for real. The stench was lustrous, and its dangerous force field threatened to pull me in like the sweet aroma of home-baked, country-style pig shit pie, and he stumbled on, ignoring the odor and closing the distance to ten feet.

I stiffened.

"Be careful, man! I'm the Pandora's box you do not want to open!" I warned him.

You should have seen his eyebrow; it was just one long, fuzzy black caterpillar stitched across his forehead. Marveling at its hideousness, I fell into a helpless trance, effectively captured by the hypnotic brow. Then, he slobbered down his fat chin, grumbled something, and hocked out a gopher-sized black loogie, which broke the spell.

I jumped back, taking notice of his *muerto*, or dead, eyes. Dark and vacant, like lifeless bird eyes, they watched without seeing. Perched behind a pair of thick, old-fashioned, black-framed glasses that were squeezed onto his pasty, round zombie face, they peered ahead, and he came on.

Plus, he still had his oil-slicked comb-over, so I thought, *what? Do you really need that now? You don't want all the other dead dudes to know you're bald? Are you kidding?* Okay, I guess I kinda understood, but he was like, a thousand years old and pretty gross, so who's gonna be cruising him, hoping for a hookup?

I didn't have time for the answer right then, because he was in range and I was about to put a punishing whack on him for trying to psyche me out with his hairstyle. Taking a quick hop for ignition, I powered toward him with the ferocity of three ADHD triplets at a birthday party after their mom leaves, nearly reaching top speed after four steps. I threw back Nine to gather killing power while putting Mr. Applebaum in my crosshairs, and just as my terrible weapon was about to release its furious energy, I tripped on something in the weeds and stumbled right past his flabby, outstretched arms and crashed headfirst into the spiked, wrought-iron fence.

Quickly, I spun around so that I was sitting with my back against the black bars, Nine still in hand. But now, reversal of fortune! Mr. Applebaum was looming over me threateningly. Drooling great, syrupy strings, he leaned in awkwardly and reached with both hands for . . . *my deal!* No way! That old zomperv was taking a run at me!

My brain exploded.

"What the cork?" I screeched. No dead zombie was gonna canoodle my pineapple. "You're one nervy son of a bitch!"

At that point, I was dealing with too many emotions to count: rage, and funny as shit—I know, he was over the line, but it looked kinda comical the way he was ogling my crotch, like a crazed diabetic kid getting into his sister's trick or treat bag when nobody's home. His lustful eyes were the size of frisbees, and he trembled with . . . lust? Oh God, he was lustful! And funny. He was fustful.

Kicking furiously at the ground, I pedaled back and away from him, scrunching up against the fence, pushing it inward a few inches. Strangely, despite the apparent danger, I couldn't keep myself from laughing at him.

When I was in fifth grade, my friends and I figured Mr. Applebaum was a chester because of the way he watched the younger kids, like a dog eyeing a cat covered in BBQ sauce. We talked about jumping him one day after detention, but then we went home to watch wrasslin' on TV instead.

Now he was like a lecherous Catholic priest running amok in a day care and I was his Communion wafer. The foul vapors that enveloped him were delightfully similar to the zombie girl's the other night, giving me that comforting feeling of warm familiarity. Shaking it off, I held my breath while my hand darted out with cobra speed to latch onto the chubby vanilla pudding wrist lunging lustily for my junk. I jerked hard and, serendipity! A sweet watch came off in my hand. Score!

After quickly pocketing my new timepiece, I jumped up to face him. He was wearing a moldy, dark blue suit jacket with brown pants. Are you kidding? Then he had on yellow socks! Does that even match? Another thing you should know is his necktie was gone, and with his top button undone, you could see wormy, gray chest fur trying to crawl out from under the neck of his dirty white dress shirt. What the hell was that about? Can you, I don't know, somehow be unaware of the muskrat rug about to leap off your flabby chest? You gotta grab some scissors and take care of that stuff, bro.

It was also obvious he'd been trying to grow a neck beard, so there's that on top of everything else. I mean, do you have to not shave the yarn growing out of your neck flab? Yeah, it's a nice look, but aren't you afraid a swingin' young mouse with an embarrassing STD might nest in there and invite his bros over to feed on the cookie crumbs? On the other hand, I guess it could have some advantages, like you wouldn't need a scarf in the winter. Or, if you're growing a bald head under your thinning hair, you could easily comb that steel wool up the sides and over the top to volumize your look.

I suppose those are good reasons, but as I studied the perverted man-beast, I couldn't stop myself from thinking about how satisfying it would be to take my hedge clippers to that furry shizz biscuit. I'd do some quick and easy manscaping, no charge.

Didn't get a chance, though. Because, although he moved with the speed of a wicked-fat kid climbing the rope in gym class, I was lost in thought, and that's when that depraved, hairy zombie took advantage and reached for my unit again.

"Are you kidding me?" I yelped. "Oh, that's it!" I was done playing. "I'm glad I ain't you cuz you're ridin' the Axeltrain now, slut! Knick-knack paddywhack, give the dog a boner!"

Like a bullet, I shot out my right hand to throttle his flabby, furry throat. I pretty much have Superman grip strength, so when I clamped down, stuff crackled inside his neck pipes, and it was gross. His saggy arms flapped around oafishly, lightly slapping up against my arm, offering basically zero resistance. God, he had the strength of a school nurse! He must have known it too, because he tried a new tactic. Angling his head down and to the side, he attempted to chomp on my death lock with his cracked brown teeth.

"Hey!" I reminded him. "Don't bite the hand that chokes you!"

Once again, he stretched out his useless noodle limbs, this time groping for my face. When I saw those knurled, yellow claws coming at me, I dropped Nine and latched on to one of his girly hands, savagely jerking it away with the rage of a fatigued new mother with yet another vile diaper.

At first, I couldn't believe it.

I blinked and looked again—yup, I had practically torn that old hand right off! It dangled down beside his knee, attached only by a long, stretchy rubber band of skin. Releasing his throat, which was now shriveled jerky, I stepped back and looked him over, wondering what else might come off. So far, I got a watch and nearly a hand. Could use a stuffed wallet . . .

When I let him go, the decrepit old bastard lost his balance, reeling backward so hard he almost fell over. After righting himself, his big barrel head turned and bent downward curiously to study his floppy hand. Shockingly, he reached over with the good one and wrenched off the useless mitt, then he tossed it to the side like a used-up *Hustler* magazine.

"Litterbug!" I hollered. "I will defeat you and take your woman as my own!" Gripping Nine in both hands, I stepped into him. "Stand tall, sir, that I might firmly smite thine foul asseth!"

I zeroed in on his square billboard forehead and took a

colossal swing. When I domed that bastard, a mighty ring echoed through the countryside, signaling to the villagers that a good thing had been done. But man, did it hurt! It was like hitting a telephone pole. With a head on it.

Instantly, angry stinging started in my hands and zinged up to my shoulders. And guess what? His old beach ball shot right off its neck moorings, lame black glasses and everything! It clanged off the fence for a standup double. Sweet!

Then I realized something: two zombie fights, two heads disconnected. Get outta here! Those zombie guys oughta think about getting some of those Frankenstein neck bolts.

Gazing with satisfaction at the still-standing, headless body, I cheered and disparaged it mercilessly with flashback revenge. "Yeah! You just got Axhandeled! How ya liking your new zombie haircut—just a little off the top! Ha-ha! Who once wet his pants during recess now, Mr. Applebaum?"

Unbelievably, the saggy body didn't fall over; it remained upright, tottering arrogantly. It taunted me by quivering and acting macho, as if nothing had happened and it was tougher than me. That part infuriated me, because who wants to be mocked by a headless body? Not me, so there's your answer.

I did the only thing I could do. With venomous fury, I roundhoused him in his deserving zombie shakers. The outrageous impact caused him to shudder and wobble before doubling over. A second later, he abruptly sprang up, stiff as a ladder, and a massive geyser of thick, blackish syrup volcanoed out of his neck hole. The glorious, brackish fountain spewed heavenward, a thousand feet or more. When it ran out of juice, that massive old body convulsed violently and toppled backward. I watched as it crashed onto its back in the grass.

I can tell you, I've taken a few nut shots myself, and I've had the pleasure of giving out several thousand, but I'd never seen that kind of reaction before. That was a good feeling. I think I kicked his balls off, and for that I was grateful.

I stood there for a little while longer, watching and waiting for whatever came next. But the body just curled up with its legs in its chest, clutching its demoralized crotch with its stump. It wasn't showing any desire to answer the bell for the next round, so when a couple minutes passed and it still hadn't moved, I was declared the winner by knockout. That's what you get for quitting. What a loser.

Suddenly, I was aware of jubilant whooping and hollering coming from the house. I whirled to see Ma in the doorway, cheering me on under the yellow porch light. I hadn't noticed it before, but powerful Misfits amperage surged from the living room speakers like it was Ozzfest. Ma was standing there eating macaroni toast and waving a giant red #1 foam finger and laughing like crazy, and that's when I knew that I was the real #1, not Mr. Applebaum.

Probably thirty-five dillion moths were fluttering around the yellow bulb above Ma's head. What's their deal? Every night they're drawn to the light like they've never seen anything like it, and they're mysticized. The next night they come back and do it all over again, pretending it's their first time. Obviously, their strategy is to skitter around it while encouraging their friends to join in and form a mosh pit. Feverishly, they fly in mad laps, circling the light while knocking into each other and occasionally bouncing off their bulb god with a tiny *tick*.

I raised my arms like I'd just won the championship wrasslin' title of the world, which I could, so it counts. When I finished my celebration dance, I thought of that dillrod Applebaum and his flying head, and I walked over to see where it might have landed. A minute later I spotted it, and yup, there was that wily raccoon, sitting smugly on top of the comb-over, smirking at me. Then, wait a minute! Was he wearing Mr. A's old black glasses?!

At first, I was proud of him, but then I stopped suddenly. Squinting hard through the murkiness, it looked like a tiny, furry middle finger was sticking straight up at me. *Son of a bitch!*

Straining harder and feeling my fury rise, I peered feverishly into the damnable darkness, forcing my eyes to see the truth. No use, I still couldn't tell. Just to be safe, I flipped off that little kinkajou. That made about the third time I've had to give the bird to one of nature's wildlives. What a bunch of asses!

I'd had enough. Aggravated, I headed for the back door. As I strolled across the yard, I sidestepped that zombie girl's head, which was surprisingly good at tripping people in the dark. Ma was just inside the door and looking puzzled when I got there.

"What's the deal with you and that raccoon?" she asked knowingly.

"That masked bandit was talking shit," I spat and closed the door.

"Raccoon this time, huh?" she asked. "What's that make, four?"

"Three," I corrected her.

Feeling a bit worn out, I put my back against the door and slowly slid down to the kitchen floor. I figured I'd rest there a bit while preventing any nighttime troublemakers from attempting an unlawful entry. Tiredly, I reached up and pulled down the mangled, ripped-up box of chocolate donuts from the edge of the table. Clearly, somebody had wanted a donut pretty damn bad and eschewed the easy way to get in.

Slumped there on the floor, I stuffed half of one of the succulent treats in my mouth, feeling its chocolaty goodness surging through me, restoring my strength.

Then Ma was standing over me, smirking.

"You wanna explain that to me, hon?" Her arms were crossed and she raised her eyebrows expectantly like moms do. She wasn't going to let it go.

"I told you, that vile little bastard is playing me, Ma. And it's only the third time—not four."

In a calm voice she said, "No, not that. The vicious-ass beating you just gave your old reading teacher."

"He taught math, Ma, and he had it coming. No sweat, it's Handeled."

I was out of air, so I stopped chewing and swallowed. Relaxing now, I took a couple of deep breaths, figuring that was the end of it. I was about to shove the rest of the donut in, but Ma was watching me, waiting for more.

"You know what, Ma? Let's just back off on the beating thing, okay? We're not here to point fingers. Besides, everyone knows it's not my fault when that happens. We agreed to call it a character flaw, remember? And if it makes you feel any better, I got injured out there in that rumble."

Ma grinned a little. "You got injured? From scrapping with that old reading teacher?" She started chuckling in a mean way.

"Ma! It hurts!" I told her, suddenly finding it hard to catch my breath.

"What hurts?"

"My leg," I gasped. "My leg!"

"Where does your leg hurt?"

"Right where you're standing on it!" I croaked.

She looked down and quickly stepped off my shin wound, which stopped hurting right about then. I must have gotten it from that stupid tripping head. I pulled myself up to my feet to prevent further damage as Ma sidled into the living room, where she sat down on the end of the couch, looking over her shoulder at me while concentrating on her next thought.

"Axel," she said, "it's just that, what you did out there was, whaddyacall . . . bad." She was doing the mom thing, trying to get me to understand something I didn't even understand.

I was puzzled. "You mean bad as in good? Because I only

deliver 'em—I don't order 'em. Besides, Mr. Applebaum just helped me get caught up on my ass kickings this week."

"Axel, you're like family to me, and I'd hate to have to replace you with one of those raggedy-ass zombies out there," Ma sighed as she topped off her glass of root beer and bit into another slice of macaroni toast.

"Ma," I reminded her patiently, "I am your family." Groaning, I limped over to the recliner and settled in, feeling more tired now.

"No, no. I really mean it, Axel. You're like a son to me," she said encouragingly. "I just don't know what I'm going to do."

"About what?"

"About finding a zombie replacement. I mean, he has to fit your clothes, and what if he doesn't like the playlists on your MP3 player?"

"Ma!"

"Quiet now," she said cuz she was done.

8

WE GOT ZOMBIES ON THE LAWN AGAIN, MA

The next night, I was watching this fishing show, and they caught a giant stingray, but it looked more like a slippery, brown, rubber tablecloth, so that's not even a fish. How can a big, flat tablecloth be a fish? But the funny part was when they pulled the tablecloth up next to the boat and it whipped its tail around, smacking the one dude with no shirt in the side of the head, knocking off his $200 sunglasses and white baseball cap.

"Wrong choice of headgear, bubba," Ma said. "You need a helmet."

"I don't know, Ma," I said. "Helmets can be dangerous. I got injured by a helmet once. Actually, it was by a guy wearing a helmet. That's why I don't believe in helmets anymore."

"I don't remember that. What happened?"

"It was in a hockey game, and I wasn't wearing a helmet. Well, the puck goes behind our goal and I skate in after it, with

Brian Klegsong right behind me. As I'm cutting around the net, he's all over me—I'm wearing him like acne on a tenth-grader. Next thing I know, his face is right next to mine as we take the corner together at a hundred miles an hour.

"Problem is, he's wearing a helmet with a wire cage on the front, and it mashes into my right ear. I got the puck, but my ear got flattened out and cut up pretty good. I vowed right then to never wear a helmet again."

"You said you weren't wearing a helmet."

"Never again."

"But, wouldn't your ear have been protected if you'd been wearing a helmet?"

"Like I said, never again," I answered, shaking my head.

"Oh."

"Afterward, I went after Brian Klegsong when he was on the bench and punched him in the ear to even things out. Then I took his girlfriend, Natalie Felcher, to dinner. Only, he wasn't on the bench when I got him—he was in his mother's driveway. And I didn't take Natalie Felcher to dinner—it was Zenobia, and we went to a movie. So that finally clears up all the confusion. Plus, Zenobia called me the next day to ask me out, but I couldn't because I had plans. Only, I didn't have plans and I ended up going out with her again."

"That's nice," Ma said in her faraway voice, which told me she'd stopped listening, so her loss.

Anyway, during the commercial break, I got up to relieve the severe wiz pressure that had beset me. As I passed by the back door, I glanced out the top window and, dammit, there was movement in the shadows near the side of the house! I took a second glimpse and, yup, I saw a group of undead corkers doing their fitful, dead-guy bop like it was slow motion night for the recklessly uncoordinated.

For some of them, the simple act of walking required every

bit of effort left in their decrepit bodies. A few were clearly disadvantaged, trying to walk on disastrously bent or torn-up legs, yet they were giving it their best so I gave them credit. It started me wondering what their motivation was, though. Somehow, it seemed, nighttime had called them out. But to do what? It was quarter to eleven at night and we had a massive overload of mindless numbnuts gathering in our yard, searching for . . . something.

You know how, when you're standing in line at the inconvenience store silently criticizing the dickhead in front of you, you realize the line's not moving? You scan ahead and see Brandi, the cashier, twirling her hair and leaning leisurely against the counter, waiting for the manager to arrive and authorize a check or something.

A couple minutes pass, and after starting out as a real trooper, your patience turns to annoyance, and then it begins to tornado into rage. Calling on all your reserves, you manage to force yourself to slow down and just breathe.

It took superhuman strength to hold back your fury, but really, think about it: if you weren't standing in line, what would you be doing with those precious three-and-a-half minutes and twelve seconds anyway? Drinking four cans of cherry cola and . . . what? Curing cancer? Come on, man. Hit the calm button.

Well, those are the same feelings I had as I looked out at those clumsy trespassers ruminating around in our yard. The thing was, I was starting to feel like I was never getting to the front of that line, cuz it looked like this bakery wasn't ever gonna close, boss. And I wasn't feeling too calm.

Now, did I wake up yesterday morning thinking I was going to get into a fight with my dead fifth-grade perv teacher and knock his head completely off with Nine? Well, I'll tell you, usually you don't see this shit coming, but I ain't going to lie to you—yes, I had a feeling something like that was going to happen. Just one of those weird feelings, I guess.

And the mob of zombie bozos shambling around outside right now? Yeah, I suppose I must have known that was going to happen somehow too—otherwise I wouldn't have written a book about it.

Ma was on the couch, glued to the TV and that stupid stingray, which they kept calling a fish. But look at it. Does that look like a fish? Even a little? You know the answer to that clown question.

I didn't want to alarm her, so, while keeping my gaze on the intruders in the yard, I said quietly, "We got zombies on the lawn again, Ma."

"That's the pot calling the pedal back," she whispered intensely, right next to my ear.

"WAAHH!" I screamed, startled out of my mind. Obviously, she didn't care if she gave me heart thrombosis. How did she get there so fast?

"What the hokey-pokey is going on around here, Ax?" She held the curtains back an inch or two and was staring fixedly into the yard with crazy eyes.

Nodding, I said, "Right on, Ma," because there's only one thing to do in a situation like that. I turned and picked up my zombie stick and headed to the door, cuz that was my unguarded rope swing out there.

When I flew out onto the porch with Nine in hand and leaped down the steps, I didn't know what to expect. But I wasn't going to think about it too hard because it was time to get that crazy monkey on, so damn the torpedoes! I zipped out onto the grass ass-fast and was surprised to see three dudes turn swiftly to face me. Given their greenish-blue hue, mucky appearance, and intoxicatingly fetid tang, it was immediately clear these guys had skipped bath night. Or they were dead.

But here's the unusual part. There was a crazy-ass-looking bulldog with them, wearing dark shades and sitting on a beat-up mini-chopper. His whitish fur was filthy and splotchy, and several bare, light gray skin patches were covered with festering sores and wriggling maggots, making it look like his flesh was moving. Not surprisingly, I suppose, he didn't seem to mind and just sat there, acting tough with his mangled half-tongue hanging out over his grimy, shriveled bottom lip.

Stopping a few feet away, I glared menacingly at them. "Hey, assbastards! You wanna back away from that rope swing before I drop you back in the shitbox you came from?"

The one in the middle, a thickset guy of about sixty and wearing a heavily stained brown pinstriped suit and about eight flashy rings on each finger, slowly turns to me and purrs real smoothly, "Watch your mouth there, slim." Talking zombies? Gnarly! His blue and white-striped necktie has been partially chewed off, and he's got an unlit skinny brown cigarette dangling from the corner of his tightly clenched mouth, and when I see that, I'm really pissed, cuz that's just unnecessary.

Feeling like I'm about to ignite, I yell, "You did not just say that, shit-for-brains! You want trouble? You dialed the right number, *boca de gusano*—maggot mouth! Let's disco!" Shaking with rage, I rear back with Nine, about to take his head off.

The dude never moves, just looks me straight in the eye and says evenly, "Okay, here's what's going to happen. You're going to put down the stick and listen very carefully. You got a problem here and we are the answer. You listenin'?"

I'm in my battle stance, but none of them have even flinched, like they know I'm not going to swing on them. How could they know that? Because the truth is, I *am* about to crack open those grinning melons. Those are some confident motherphuckers! Reconsidering, I slowly bring Nine to my shoulder and step forward, so we're a couple feet apart.

Calmly, the talking one commandingly tilts his head back and rumbles throatily, "The name's Mikey Killzitti. These here are my, ah, associates." His face is bloated, and his skin is papery and sloughing. The greasy silver hair on his head is soiled and thick and as impenetrable as Dad's cookie cupboard. He turns slightly and waves an arm indifferently in the direction of the others. "That's Slashski Rodriguez. He . . . slashes stuff. And shoots stuff."

"With a gun," Slashski giggles hoarsely, "and a knife." He's a solid six feet tall, maybe two hundred pounds, no potbelly, slicked black hair, and maybe fifty years old. He's wearing a rumpled gray suit, and one hand rests just above his belt, while the other is hovering slightly behind his back.

"Right," continues Mikey. He motions to the other dude. "That there, that's Vinnie Two Eyes. He sees things."

It looks like Vinnie's huge gray saucer eyes are fixed in a stare, but that's just because his damn eyelids are gone. And because he stares at things.

"I see everything you are thinking," hisses Vinnie, sounding like a scary Halloween gypsy fortunate teller. His brow is furrowed, like he's concentrating while trying to appear menacing. He glares out across the yard, not even looking at me. He's maybe thirty-five, wiry, and rodent-looking in a dark blue suit. Thin gray lips and flared nostrils sit low upon his long rectangular face, and his left hand appears to have been hacked off, leaving a mangled white stub of arm bone hanging an inch past the sleeve of his suit coat. It's been whittled down to the size of a finger, and it's wearing a gold ring with a big ruby sitting in the middle.

"Is that so?" I say, staring straight at Vinnie and leaning forward. "Then you must see me putting you in the truth lock, which exerts such outrageous abuse on your system you'll confess to shit you never even knew about." Unaffected,

Vinnie turns and gazes hungrily at me like I'm the worm and he's the trout, and Mikey continues.

"This here," Mikey says, gesturing to the bulldog sitting on a little motorcycle and wearing a black leather vest with a tiny skull and crossbones patch on the shoulder, "is Trey. Trey does . . . special things for us, don't you, Trey?"

"Dat's right, Boss," the dog growls, glancing briefly up at Mikey. Then he throws off his shades, jumps down, and purposefully waddles over to me.

"Dey calls me Trey, cuz dat's another language for t'ree," he croaks thickly. His teeth are worn down to little brown corn kernels, probably from chewing on bones or softening leather—human leather, I bet. His faded brown eyes are sunken way back into his little square dog head, and I see he's got a tribal tattoo on his left foreleg—who tattoos a damn dog?

My mouth's probably hanging open because it's a talking dog, but I'm curious about something.

"Yeah, it's Spanish for 'three,' " I tell him. "But why do they call you a number?" I'm watching and trying not to giggle.

"Cuz I gots t'ree legs," he snarls, low and guttural.

Now, I can clearly see he has all four legs, so I'm not sure what to think. I can't help staring, and I rapidly count the legs probably seventeen times, and each time I come up with four.

"You know," I say carefully, "I can see——"

"Hey, look at you!" he growls. "You can see. Well, isn't dat somethin'? So yer a smart guy, den." This son of a bitch is sarcastic.

"Here's something," I say cheerfully and flash a big smile at him. "For a dead dog, you smell a lot like a dead dog. With a dead dog's ass. That reeks like ass. Dead ass. Ass that's dead."

He tenses, and when his eyes narrow, he utters a sinister grating growl. "You a smart guy? Whud ya do, go to school, den?"

"Yeah," I confess, cuz I never talked to a zombie dog before and didn't know how stupid he was for sure.

"I went to school once," he chortles. "I'll tell ya dis much: dat Mrs. What's-her-not, she got herself a nice, long time-out in da corner, eh boys? Ssst ssst ssst," he whisper-laughs, glancing over at his colleagues. "Shoulda been nicer to da kids—'specially da Boss's kid. Ssst ssst ssst."

I grin and ask, "She didn't know he was the Boss's kid?"

Trey snarls at me. "Hey! Was I talkin' to you?"

"Uh, I think so," I stammer.

"Shut it, kid, you're startin' to give me lassitude."

This dog is asking for a good nut kicking, but I decide to let it go and shift gears so I can try to get some information.

"So, are you a zombie dog?"

He doesn't even look at me. "You aksin me a question?"

"No," I say quietly, then, "*are* you?"

"Listen, da ting about me is I may be dead—but I ain't alive neither, unnerstan', punk?"

"Yeah. So, Trey—"

"What'd you call me?" he snarls.

I blink. "Trey?"

"Dat's better," he huffs. "Don't be bustin' my balls, kid." He sounds funny and looks funny, but he also looks like he wants my leg bone.

Cautiously, I try again. "No, ah, you look like a, uh . . . what kind of dog are you?"

"You wanna know? You sure you wanna know?"

I wasn't sure. "What could happen if I did know?"

"Tings. Tings could happen. You want dat, kid?" he says threateningly.

"Well, no. Unless one of the things is chocolate pudding."

"So now you're a wise-ass? You a wise-ass punk now?"

"I like chocolate pudding."

"Don't be bustin' my twinklers, kid," Trey growls. "Don't do it."

I give him my best innocent look. "I won't."

A murderous grin creases his greasy dog lips. "So, den, you seen Tony?"

"Tony?"

"Don't do it, kid," he snaps angrily. "Don't twist my knobs."

"Uh, yeah, I saw Tony."

"And you told him?" he demands.

"Yeah, sure. I told him—I told Tony," I splutter.

Then he blows his top. *"You told Tony?* You outa ya mind? What da hell's wrong wit' choo?!"

That little tattooed dog with dirty white fur is furiously shaking his scruffy head from side to side, throwing thick ropes of amber-colored drool over everybody's shoes.

Confused, I say frantically, "I thought you wanted me to tell Tony."

"You gotta lot ta learn, kid," he blisters, shaking his head. A long moment passes before he continues, more composed this time. "Tell ya what I'ma gonna do. I'ma help you out dis one time, but dat's it, unnerstan'?"

My heart is thumping as I say, "No. I don't even know no Tony. I just thought that's what you wanted to hear." I'm starting to feel a little unsettled, so I grip Nine tighter, and wait.

He starts chuckling. "Dat's all right, kid, dare ain't no Tony. I was just testing ya. Ya did all right. Ssst ssst ssst."

"You gonna tell Tony?" I ask him.

His little grin disappears. "You gonna get me a glazed donut before I sharpen my teeth on your pole?"

"A glazed donut?" I ask.

"It's funny," he muses, looking around, bewildered, "I know I said it, because I felt da words go in my ears, but I still don't see no glazed donut." Now he seems upset as he saunters toward me on those wide, bent legs. "How about if I go Cujo on your Mr. Tallywhacker and his two chimes? Will I get my donut den, do ya tink? Huh?" He's getting worked up.

"That's enough, Trey," orders Mikey, patiently. "Look kid, we're here on business."

"Yeah, bithnith," spews Slashski, scowling and grinning while patting the front of his jacket like he's got something important under there.

Instantly, I focus on Slashski.

"No way!" I exclaim. "Dude, did you just say bithnith?"

"No," mutters Slashski timidly, his smile disappearing.

"Yes, you did, I heard you!" I chuckle.

His face turns deathly dark. "I didn't thay that!" he protests angrily.

"There! You did it again!" Now I'm laughing out loud. "Jeez, man, you ever heard of speech therapy? What are you, six?" I can see he's really embarrassed and fuming, so I re-grip Nine, because something's coming.

"You think that'th funny?" he says menacingly while easily slipping one hand into the breast pocket of his jacket. "How'd you like a knife in the eye?" Wearing a sinister leer, he's shuddering with rage as he studies me.

"Just hold on now." I put up my free hand to Slashski. Then in a serious tone, I ask him, "Where would the knife go again?"

Making an angry gurgling sound, he eyes me up and down and shuffles calculatingly toward me.

"Wait," I go on, "did you say a knife or a pipe in the eye? And is that a tobacco pipe? Because I don't smoke. Although, I have been thinking about taking up a hobby . . ." I think for a second. "Okay. Sure, I'll go with the pipe; it's not as sharp is it? But can it be one of those pipes that blows bubbles? Those are cool. Do you have any purple ones? Oh, and can you make sure none of the soap gets in my eye—that stings."

Vinnie's wide, unblinking eyes bore holes into me as he steps in front of the crazed knifer. "I can see him getting two knives in the eye, Boss," he hisses, holding back Slashski and gazing hard at me while grinding his teeth through an evil grin.

"Hmm," I consider, turning my attention to Vinnie. "Can you see me giving you a haircut? Look hard, maybe you can see it. It'll be just like at the barbershop, I promise. Only not as relaxing. And without the haircutting. It'll be more like eating a ham sandwich, only with no ham, cuz it's Lent. But it still has the bread, and in between the bread is my meaty fist."

"All right, kid," deadpans Mikey impatiently. He hasn't moved an inch since I first approached them. "Look, we're here to help. You got rats scurrying around this place. We're here to take care of 'em."

I turn to Mikey, curious now. "You're going to remove the zombies?"

"No. Like I said, we're here to help you with your rat problem."

"Rat problem?"

"It's like dis, kid," explains Trey. "Ya gots good zombies and ya gots rats. Da rats are ours—don't touch 'em. Dat's what we're here for. Got it?"

"How can you tell a good zombie from a rat zombie?" I ask.

"Vinnie," boasts Mikey, and motions to the wide-eyed psychopath.

"I see 'em. I see 'em all." Vinnie's nodding fervently, and his face is completely blank as he examines the four or five shamblers wandering near us.

Oddly wistful, Mikey sighs, "My mother always said if you're gonna go outside in the rain, don't drink the wine." With a calm expression, he appears to be contemplating while gazing up into the dark sky.

"Rain," slurs Slashski.

"Wine," adds Vinnie.

"Okay," I mutter because I don't know what the hell that means.

I shake my head a little to try to clear it, because none of this really seems to make sense, and that last part was just stupid. I mean, these guys are zombie hunters, which is a little strange since they seem to be zombies also, but they're prejudiced against zombies—well, certain bad zombies, as they tell it. So now, I'm mulling it over, and it comes to me: I think I know who they really are!

"Hey," I start out delicately, "how come you guys are . . . zombies, right? But you're still doing what you did before?"

Mikey sets his jaw and his eyes harden. "Spit it out, kid."

"Well, it's just that," I say, lowering my voice, "you're talking about, you know, eliminating guys—but only certain guys. Like a hit squad, or . . . it sounds like . . . mob activity." I whisper the last two words.

Immediately, Vinnie, large-eyed, steps forward and flies off the handle. "What are you, the guy what asks the questions? Should we just call you the Question Asking Guy? Would you like that?"

"Sure, that doesn't sound too bad." I say, nodding. "Or Ace. I've always wanted to be called Ace."

"Oh yeah? Well, how you gonna athk quethtionth wit' yer mout' thlathed off?" Slashski says threateningly.

"You talk funny," I say and start giggling again. Then I compose myself, look down, and think for a second. "Hold on. I don't know . . . you mean my lips?"

"Do you want that?" chirps Slashski, about as excited as a dog on a mailman sundae. "You want your lipth thlathed off?"

"Well, I mean, how would you do it?"

"Do what?" smiles Slashski, leaning forward and looking very interested.

"Cut someone's mouth off. I'm just wondering how you would do it."

"You don't think I could do it?" sneers Slashski as he slowly, almost lovingly, slides out a long, rusty knife with no handle.

"No, I don't think so . . . no."

"What, did you go to high school or something, kid?" Mikey pipes in.

"No," I shrug. "I just don't see how anyone could cut off a person's mouth, that's all. You got the lips and the jaws and bones and stuff. How would you do all that?"

"You want I should teach you? Now I'm your teacher?" Mikey bellows, all wise-assed.

"Are you a good teacher?" I say. "Should I call you Professor Mikey?"

"Look here," Mikey sniffs real importantly while running his thick, rotting hand down the front of his jacket to smooth out a million deep wrinkles, but it doesn't smooth. "Some of the boys here, they might refer to me as the Dogfather. It's a term of endearment, you might say. So let's leave that be. Now, as for you," he points a ragged finger at my chest, "I ain't got no time to be teaching some punk kid about our ways, that's what."

"What ways? You have ways?" I ask.

"We got ways, yeah," hisses Vinnie, smiling malevolently.

"Sweet." I'm smiling right back now.

"We ain't teaching you though," Mikey spits.

"What, I'm not good enough for you?"

"Kid, you're not good enough for anybody," says Mikey coldly.

"You could teach me if you wanted to."

"No, I couldn't."

I press on. "What if you wanted to? Then you would."

"That'd be different. Then I would teach you."

"No thanks—I gotta do some stuff." I look at my watch. "And I should watch some TV, too."

"I didn't say I was going to teach you," huffs Professor Mikey with an attitude. Some teacher.

"You were hinting around at it though, and I don't like to be pressured." I shake my head. "Thanks anyway." I relax my grip on Nine and look around, surveying the growing zombie activity in the yard.

"Don't look now, but I see something," rasps Vinnie, staring intently toward the cemetery.

"I don't see anything unusual," I say, glancing around through the growing darkness.

"You ain't Vinnie Two Eyes, punk," growls Trey.

"If you could see what I see, you'd think you were seeing things," snaps Vinnie in a low, sinister voice. "Wait. Listen . . . I see footsteps." He's squinting real hard across the yard. "Did you see that?"

"No," I say impatiently.

"I just saw what you're thinking." Now he's looking at me knowingly, grinning crazily like he has a secret.

"Can you always see what I'm thinking?" I ask.

"Yes."

"What if I'm actually thinking about something else?"

"Then I can't see it."

I figure that's just about enough nonsense, because now I'm bored. And hungry.

"All right, fellas," I sigh, "I'm going inside for a snack now."

Mikey muses softly, "The man who receives a cannoli is a man who knows much."

"Cannoli," slurs Slashski.

"Much," adds Vinnie.

"Yeah, I don't know what the hell that means either, so I'm gonna go," I snap, starting to feel downright annoyed.

"To become one with the spaghetti sauce, one must walk the path," contemplates Mikey, in his million-miles-away voice.

"Thauth," slurs Slashski.

"Path," adds Vinnie.

"And, there's another one," I grumble irritably, because Mikey's puzzling philosophical sayings are pushing me toward unchecked violence. Then I get an idea. "Hey, I almost forgot. Tomorrow I'm having a zombie barbecue, and I invited my friends, who I hate. We're gonna have zombie burgers, with bits of real zombies, so you know they're good and they're the real thing. You boys are welcome to come over—I might need you . . . if I run out, that is," I say to piss them off.

"It has recently come to my detention that you've been very lippy today, kid," replies Mikey in what must be his deep, tough-guy voice.

"Real lippy," snarls Trey shuffling forward.

"You need to watch yourthelf," scowls Slashski lispily, waving his big knife around in a figure eight. "I have anger problemth."

I slap Nine into the palm of my hand.

"Hey, Slash," I say, "why do you work so hard to be a dickhead? Let it come naturally. Relax, man, it'll come." I'm getting real tired of his threats.

He winces and raises the knife to throat level, twelve inches away from my neck. Quickly, Mikey holds his arm across Slashski's chest to stop him. Slashski has this four-inch scar racing across his forehead that's flaring like a set of monkey balls in a poison ivy loincloth.

"That'th a cute little baby bat, Little Leaguer," Slashski chuckles meanly.

"I got it at your mom's house," I reply.

"THON OF A BITCH!" he screams and tries to charge, but Mikey's holding him back.

I stare down Slashski.

"The fist is anger's best friend," I say, "and I got at least two of 'em, so think about that, girls!" I study their faces. The dog looks like he wants my ankle marrow, and I notice they've all moved forward slightly. "You fellas gonna go big boy on me now? Tell you what I'm going to do. First, let's pretend I haven't kicked your ridiculous asses yet."

"You haven't kicked my ath yet," sneers Slashski, itching for a fight.

"Ha! You said 'yet,' which means you just admitted that I'm going to," I gloat victoriously. "So, let's just say that I haven't yet. What makes you think you're going to escape a beating?" I start pacing back and forth in front of them like that lawyer guy on that show. "Tell you what I'm going to do. First, I'm going airborne for two minutes, and while I'm up there, I'm getting you in a chokehold with my feet and ordering a large pepperoni pizza on my phone. Want a slice? Too bad, there's not enough to go around." I'm staring right at Slashski.

"Don't try it, kid," threatens Mikey, shifting. "You're talking crazy."

I smirk. "Oh yeah? Tell you what I'm going to do. First—"

"Stop sayin' 'tell ya what I'm gonna do'!" screams Vinnie.

"Is that a fact?" I jeer, calmly. "Now you went and did it. You really did it this time. This time you had to go and really do it. You just had to go and do it, didn't you? You really went—"

"All right, already!" roars Slashski, who by now is nothing short of bloodthirsty. "Thut up with that thit! I'm gonna carve my name on your ath!" His knife slashes through the air and he's ready to go.

"Will that make you my girlfriend?" I ask him sweetly.

Convulsing with rage, he snarls, "Thith kid ith getting me all thlathy!" His knife is waving around like he can't control it.

"Tell you what I'm going to do," I explain. "First, I'm going to hit you so hard all the colors will get mixed up, making the sky green and the grass blue, and you'll look down and think you're in the ocean and you'll drown from your own fright because you never learned to swim. Then, congratulations! You just won two free tickets to Axelmania, dude. Bring a friend to this year's big festival in my backyard, as my guests. As soon as you arrive, show your tickets to Juan and you'll get upgraded to VIP, where you won't have to stand in line—I'll kick your ass right away, no waiting. Then, as an added bonus, I'll make your friend cry. What do you say?"

For a minute, there's nothing but dumbfounded silence.

"Are you out of your mind, kid?" bristles Mikey, finally.

"Maybe I am, or maybe you're out of my mind. There's just one thing," I say cheerfully, gazing at each one. "I'm going to need a special favor from you. When the beating starts, keep me updated on the progress, because sometimes when I'm rumbling, I blank out. Don't worry, I'll keep pummeling you, it's just that I don't get to see the destruction until it's over. Describe your beatings to me as I baste you so I can enjoy it more. Unless you videotape it. Who has a camera?"

"Dat's crazy, punk," snarls Trey.

I smile down at him. "And don't be coming at me for no dog biscuits, Lassie. If I can't eat 'em, neither should you. The last time, I ate a whole box and they went straight to my heart and gave me a blood clog."

"You mean blood clot?" asks Mikey.

"No, first my heart—and then my stomach—got clogged up and I couldn't eat anymore. I had to do eleven sit-ups before I could shove down another half a box."

"That ain't no blood clot," hisses Vinnie.

"Were you there, Dr. Quinn, Medicine Woman?" I say.

"Game on!" Vinnie fires back and steps into me.

"Let's bam!" I scream while taking a fighting stance, and they all jump back, out of range. "I'm coming at you idiots like a castrated jungle monkey." I'm swinging Nine slowly back and forth in fighting rhythm. "Somebody's about to get Nined."

"Put the knife down, Slashski," orders Mikey calmly. Slashski looks at him disbelievingly for about five seconds, then he pockets the nine-inch sticker and glares at me.

The others back up a couple more steps and relax. The show's over. One thing's for sure, these guys sure don't like you messing with them. They must have really been something when they were alive. Still, I figure I've got to mess with them one last time, so I rest Nine on my shoulder and take a friendly posture and tone of voice.

"Hey, listen. I know why you guys are so testy. I get that you're into chicks *and* dudes, but being bilingual doesn't give you a free pass. If you're going to get all PMS with me, you're gonna need two of Axel's Killing Pills. Side effects include pain, missing limbs, and deep shame. Oh, and did I mention the killing part? There's a killing part. It comes at the end. Now, you boys want a free prescription?"

Mikey stiffens and sourly glares past me at something.

"Listen, kid, we didn't come here for you. We got other plans," he grumbles.

He makes a subtle hand gesture, and with that, his gang wordlessly turns and shambles away, not looking back.

Apprehensively, I check behind me, but there's nothing there in the darkness, so I think it was a bluff. He probably faked it because he was scared of Nine and was trying to shave face in front of his friends.

Zombie mobsters.

Chickenshits.

9
DON'T LOOK AT ME WITH THAT HAIR

A few nights later, it was starting to get late when Ma shuffled off to bed and left me listening to a crew of mad zombies abusing our house. I didn't feel like sleeping, so I went into the bathroom with my BB gun. Carefully, I slid the small window up and removed the screen. Standing beside the commode with my head halfway out the window, I had a good view of the backyard scene in the moonlight. There wasn't nearly as much scratching and caterwauling going on back there, just half a dozen mindless drifters moping around the yard. None of those monkeys saw me, so I aimed at a guy about twelve feet away who was clumsily precipitating around in circles with a stupid, gaping look on his face.

He had dark beehive hair piled up higher than Lyle Lovett's and was wearing mismatched tennis shoes and a grubby black tuxedo, which must have been rented. Good luck getting your deposit back, bonehead. But the worst moment in my life came when I realized I hated looking at his damn squirrely face.

As I zeroed in on the lucky target, a weird shiver raced through my skeleton, making my teeth vibrate. For a frightful second I was certain that beehive shrub was staring me down. I took my finger off the trigger and pulled up, studying the hair. After what must have been two full minutes, a rogue mosquito buzzing in my ear finally broke the spell. Shaking off the powerful effects of the dude's head fur, I leveled my weapon, bringing his anvil-shaped face back into my crosshairs.

As I prepared to pull the trigger, I glanced at the hair again. There was no doubt the dude's lid was in need of a trim; that much must be made perfectly clear. His last barber must have had two eyes, and both were blind. Once more, I lowered the gun, unable to fire. That hair. There was something . . . bossy about it; it was acting like it was the king of bathroom BB gun snipers, and it was sending me a message to not do something. But what?

Gazing unblinkingly through the murk, I studied it, convinced the mane was controlling the dude, and calling to me. It had some kind of mystical power, I was sure. Determined not to succumb, I squeezed my eyes shut and recalled the promise I had made to myself years before that no damn hair was ever gonna tell me what to do again.

Raising my BB gun once more, I aimed at the zombie dude it controlled and sighted in on his idiotic face. No way could I miss from that distance. Right about then I decided to call him Grover High Hair—not the hair, the zombie, because it would be stupid to give a name to a zombie's puppetmaster hair. (Maybe you could call it Harry, or Curtis.) I held my breath and squeezed the trigger.

POP! Nailed him in the ear—I bet it zipped into that little earhole!

He swung around like he'd been shot and spotted me in the

window. Man, that dude could really see in the dark! He stumbled hungrily toward me as I calmly cocked the gun and aimed.

POP! Right in his damn eye!

He sorta pawed at the fresh ooze dripping from his eye and kept coming. He was eight feet away now, and I aimed again.

POP! I heard a sharp *crack* this time and saw a long, yellow Chiclet spin right out of his stupid mouth to the ground. Eagle eye! Took a damn tooth right out. I was jacked!

And pissed.

"Litterbug! Pick that up, skell!" I yelled softly cuz I didn't want to wake Ma. But I ain't the one who left that damn tooth there. Besides, it wasn't mine.

Of course, Grover acted like he didn't hear me and kept coming, and I started to admire that determined rat-eating son of a bitch. For fun, I plugged him again in that same liquid-jelly eye. He flinched but came steadily onward, groaning like Grandpa Daquon out on parole and drunkenly trying to get up off the couch to get another box of wine.

Next thing you know, we were locked in a fierce battle. Grover eagerly reached up and in through the little bathroom window, which wasn't easy because it's about five feet off the ground, and he wasn't much taller than that. Like a short, bad-mannered trick-or-treater, he begged for more. So I plugged him point-blank between the eyes, leaving a bright scarlet welt. Clumsily, he extended his girly arms to flail at me. Too bad for him he couldn't reach me, and the window was so small his shoulders were never going to fit through, even if he could get high enough. That looper wasn't coming in unless he had stilts, but where are you going to find stilts at that time of night?

I knew what I had to do, so I did it.

There comes a time in every man's life when he has to make a difficult decision, and none of the choices are popular. It is during those times that real men are born. Embracing that knowledge, I accepted my fate to go down in history as an unpopular hero. Aiming around his groping sissy arms, I furiously cocked and shot repeatedly. The blue steel barrel of my murderous Gatling gun grew hot and began to smoke as I scored heavily on his hideous, increasingly pulpy face, opening up dozens of raw, bloody blisters. After a couple minutes of sustained damage, he finally dragged his useless arms and face out of the window, and I figured that was the end of it.

Nope.

A second later, his gruesome, skinny head pushed into the opening, and the one good but cloudy eye zeroed in on me, lusting for meat. It seemed his new plan was to expose his face even more while he used the massive power in his scrawny stick neck to pull himself through the window and into the bathroom by his chin. What an idiot. He deserved what was coming to him.

Backing up a little in the tiny bathroom so he wouldn't bite my gun, I held the end of the barrel maybe three inches from his greasy forehead. I didn't even hafta aim. For some reason, I then rapidly began cracking fifty rounds per minute into that overconfident zombie's mug. The lethal copper BBs bounced off his face bones and ricocheted back toward me before ping-ponging around the bathroom walls. I had to stay alert—anybody will tell you those comebackers are a bitch.

Every time I shot, I heard a little *zik!* as the BB connected to his bony face, and he'd twitch and get a little more annoyed. He was game, but unfortunately, my cocking arm tired out after a few minutes, so I had to cease fire and rest. Grover's battered head was still all the way through the window—that crazy nest on top was obviously running the show, urgently driving him on to more punishment. But he was such an ineffective intruder all he could do was groan and gaze longingly at me, slobbering hopefully and whatnot.

"Aw, would you like some help?" I asked, using my nice-guy voice and smiling at him. "Here, let me help you a little."

SLAP! I monster-smacked him hard across his stupid face.

"Did that help? Let me help you some more."

SLAP! I cracked him even harder, spraying zombie blood across . . . *Ma's new shower curtain!*

"What the——?! Is that your mess on our new shower curtain?" I asked him. He didn't say nothing.

SLAP! "See what happens when you don't own up to it?"

SLAP! SLAP! A quick double-slap made him think twice about wrecking Ma's new stuff.

SLAP! SLAP! SLAP! It was hard to stop once I got started.

Leaning against the sink and watching his sluggish desperation while I wiped the gunk off my burning slapper, I saw that he must have been about thirty years old. He had a goofy, swirly black mustache and long, fuzzy muttonchop sideburns. Muttonchops? As soon as I saw those 'burns, I think I lost my mind. In an instant, I pinned his head down on the windowsill and grabbed one of Ma's supposable plastic razors off the sink. A dizzying sensation came over me, and the room filled with the sound of mad, high-pitched cackling, which thundered off the bare bathroom walls and chased itself around and around the small room.

A few seconds later, my jaws were aching, and that's when I understood that the manic laughing was coming from me. Also, I was sheering those arrogant 'burns right off Grover's nearly translucent cheeks. Right about then he blew his top and made a real effort to get away. Maybe he wanted to do the shaving himself, or maybe it was the humiliation of the pink razor, I couldn't tell.

I had no choice but to drop the razor and release him while placing the barrel of my deadly BB gat an inch from his oily forehead. Heroically, I fired off twenty searing rounds. He valiantly attempted to elude my shots by listlessly gawking at the end of the barrel and making grunting noises. His skillful defensive maneuver was ineffective however, and he continued taking a ton of hits. It must have hurt, but I couldn't be sure because he was a poor communicator. The best part was I hadn't missed my target yet. Unfortunately, after a few more minutes I got bored and it stopped being fun.

Then, as I surveyed his battered face, a curious thought occurred to me. Without hesitating, I reached out and allowed my fingertips to dance effortlessly across the tiny swollen bumps on the message board of Grover's forehead to see if I had written something clever in Braille. Maybe it was a secret zombie message, I thought excitedly.

My fingers glided feverishly over the raised dots and my anticipation rose, but it was tough reading cuz Grover wouldn't stay still. Also, I guess I don't know Braille, so I never found out what the important message said. Maybe it had something to do with hair-controlled zombies, I'll probably never know. My precision shooting had jacked up his face something wicked though, and I figured he would henceforth be known as Mr. Bumpy Face, mocked forever by the popular crowd. And the Braille-reading blind.

With my bump-reading fingers still on his roughed-up forehead, Mr. B.F. suddenly rotated his choppers upward and viciously snapped at my hand, forcing me to pull back and get aggravated. I was peeved all right; you shouldn't try to bite someone who's reading your face. Not only that, but that ingrate just got a free shave!

Purposely, I reached up over his head to the sliding window above him and slammed the sash down onto the back of his bony neck. Then I snagged the plunger from behind the toilet and jammed it up between the top of the window and the window frame above it. This effectively locked the spiteful Grover in place and made him Prisoner Number One—the first guy ever to get caught in my Polack guillotine, and making Ma's prediction come true that someday one of us Handel Polacks would capture and circumcise an intruder in the bathroom. I figured I'd stick with just the first part for now; I'm not really into that other thing.

In total control now, I zestfully grabbed a handful of that domineering shrub and yanked it upward so I could look at Grover's ruined face.

"Say you're sorry, dimbulb," I warned him. "Say it or you'll never get freedom."

Reaching behind me, I flicked on the light switch, and the tiny room exploded in brightness, causing Grover to spasm unexpectedly. He snorted like a mule, and his glassy, vacant eye danced wildly around the suddenly illuminated bathroom. But I didn't feel sorry for him cuz he had it coming. I examined his face in the light, and aside from hundreds of bloody pockmarks and one abused eyeball, it wasn't impressive.

"That's a bitchin' mustache, Grover. It almost hides your lovely, buttery-yellow teeth. Too bad for you though, cuz that 'stache is coming off unless you say you're sorry, sourbelly."

He began thrashing his revoltingly musky head around like a guy trying to get free, but that was not gonna happen. He was pinned tight. Keeping a fistful of his hair clutched in one hand, I pulled open the drawer by the sink with the other. I had to really stretch to scoop out the old straight razor that hides in there, way back behind the used-up deodorants.

"You're right. We need to glam up your look, bro," I told him encouragingly as I flashed the deadly razor in front of his ridiculous mustache.

"Nnuhh," he said.

"Don't call me that!" I screamed and wrenched his head up

to gaze into his lying eyes. "Now," I said politely, "are you sure you want to go for the Tom Cruise look? Is that the kind of commitment you feel you're ready for?"

"Nnuhh," he grunted, which must mean "go ahead" because that's what I did.

"Good choice," I agreed and quickly sliced off that dumb mustache in four strokes. Then, to surprise his family for the holidays, I took off each bushy brown eyebrow. After that, it was time for the necessary interrogation. "Did you ride on my rope swing?"

"Nnuhh," I think is what he grunted, but I wasn't sure, since I was a little closed-minded, what with my brain being clouded with rage over recent events involving my new swing.

"Did you?" I repeated.

"Nnuhh," he gurgled with bravado.

"Did you?" I said louder, madder now.

"Nnuhh," he burbled stubbornly, and I think he meant it.

I smiled. "That's right. Now, don't you feel better?" I said pleasantly.

"Nnuhh," he grumbled.

"Don't take that tone!" I snarled. "Now, I'm going to ask you again: don't you feel better for confessing?" I wanted to hear his answer because I knew he was lying.

"Nnuhh," he croaked egotistically.

"It's cards on the table time, Grover—*if* that is your real name. Tell me, did you or did you not come here looking to get into some mischief?"

"Nnuhh."

"That's better." I was satisfied. "Okay, then, it's been fun, and we'll have to do it again sometime. Hey, I know! You can be my favorite beat-monkey. How's that sounding?" I let go of his hair and stood back, assessing his style with a careful eye. "P.S., no charge for the groovy new look."

But it appeared Grover wasn't too grateful, because he just googly-eyed me and drooled all over the rug. When he started to sputter and retch, I knew the window guillotine had done its job. I pulled out the plunger and slid the window up to free him. Groggily, he lifted his eye to blaze hatefully at me. Then the lousy backstabber tried to climb in through the window again!

My fury returned, and I thought, *what the hell did I ever do to you?*

"Here, let me help you, pee pants!" I screamed.

I plunged both hands into his grubby head quills and latched on for all I was worth. A mighty upward heave stretched his pipe cleaner neck about fourteen inches and his shoulders crashed loudly into the window frame, and he squealed like a chimpanzee wearing a poison ivy jockstrap. After six or seven more hellacious jerks, which helped ease my anger, I let him go. He fell back, and his head slipped outside the window.

Finally! God, I was tired of looking at that face.

But no, we weren't done yet. Carnivorously determined, Grover High Hair's face immediately burst back through the window again. It startled me at first, then I was impressed with his fortitude. Then I got real, real mad. Grittier than ever, he began furiously clawing at the window frame, trying to widen the hole and tunnel through, I guess. I could hear his feet desperately scrabbling against the outside of the house as he frenziedly tried to climb up and in. He was grunting fiercely, and, surprisingly, he was actually beginning to force his newly busted-up and sleeker shoulders through the hole.

"What the hell!" I yelled. "Have you got a woodrow for me or something? I'm done playing, McBitch!"

I fired my fist into the middle of his face, rocking his melon viciously into the window frame, but it rebounded right back to me. Then I hammered my palm under his chin so hard his head jolted backward until his forehead actually slipped under the bottom window sash and stuck there. The back of his head was pinned against his shoulder blades, and his bulging eye was looking straight up at the bathroom ceiling. Cool trick! He couldn't hold it though, because his greasy forehead had lubricated the wood enough to allow his slimy dome to slip out of the clutches of the window trap. His liberated head sprung forward and his stupid zombie face was looking at me again.

Then, dammit! He was enthusiastically mounting another assault! Man, that guy just wouldn't quit; I thought, *I should put this rube on my hockey team.*

"Nnuhh," he said, as if that was supposed to intimidate me.

I was enraged. "Good idea, assmonkey! Come on in and let's party!"

I locked onto his hair again and kangarooed his head in toward the bathroom as hard as I could. At that moment, the only thing I ever wanted in life was to get him inside so I could beat his ass royally. With another heave, the wood around the window groaned and his slim right shoulder slid through the opening. His feet were off the ground outside, kicking wildly against the house. A shrill, agonized scream tore from his lungs like a silver defense siren, erupting so loud I worried he would wake Ma. I was getting a good response now.

Quickly, I grabbed his ears and pulled even harder. Sick, tearing noises came from where the ears attach to the skull. His arms and legs were thrashing crazily and slapping against the siding outside. Just then, I remembered that zombie girl and Mr. Applebaum, and how easily their decrepit noggins—and Mr. A's hand—came off, and it gave me an idea.

Feeling encouraged, I decided to switch my grip to a full-on guillotine choke and try to duplicate Ma's feat of plucking off a dead head. I maneuvered into position and quickly locked my opponent in the vice. The window is so high I had to place my feet on the wall below the frame to get the necessary leverage. Squeezing hard and leaning back with everything I had, my body was parallel to the floor as I cranked out thirty megatons of pressure on his neck. Wicked popping noises filled the small bathroom, inspiring me to squeeze and pull even harder. All of a sudden, when his cork was about to screw right off—you guessed it—Ma appeared right beside me.

Her eyes were sleepy but her anger wasn't.

"Ax! Stop jacking around with your new girlfriend!" she yelled from six inches away in her parking lot voice.

"But Ma, he stole my MP3 player," I protested between breaths, and I wasn't letting go.

"That's not the same zombie, Ax."

"What are you saying, Ma?" I tightened my grip a little.

"I don't know who bagged your MP3 player, but he's leaking on my floor. Let him go." She put her hands on my arms.

"So you're taking his side, then?" I re-gripped, feeling desperate and applying gorilla-ass force.

"Whose side?"

"Grover's," I said, holding my breath because of the strain.

"Who?" Her hands were on her hips and she yawned, looking edgy.

"Grover," I repeated.

Shaking her head, she said, "Who the hell is Grover?"

"Yeah, pretend you don't know. You always take his side." Angrily, I cinched it up another notch and hastily gulped in a few mouthfuls of air. Grover was spluttering and dripping goo, and his pop-top was close to coming off.

Gently, Ma put an arm around my shoulder. "Ax, just because I rock doesn't mean I'm made of stone. I hear your inner pain coming through my heart headphones." With a hand on her heart, she looked kind of hurt. "I'm sorry for your loss, but we'll get it back."

I thought about it for a second and realized she was probably right. I relaxed some and nodded. "Ma, you're a genius."

"That's what my business card says."

So, I let go of Grover, whose gooey face slapped noisily onto the windowsill before he lifted it up to look at us. His blank cyclops-gaze pivoted from Ma to me. Then, to his credit, he tried to scramble through the window again! Only this time—despite the damage I'd put on him—with more gusto.

For a second I felt bad for him. "Hey, assface, don't be mad at me because you can't get a date—I did my part to spruce you up."

He pulled his head out and poked his clumsy arms through yet again. Then he started wildly whipping those skinny sticks around inside the bathroom with the embarrassing strength of a professional golfer. Bitterly, I thought about breaking them off when I noticed a sweet, innocent sports watch staring at me. How did I miss that before? In a flash, I moved in and gripped his skinny, leathery forearm with one hand and doinked the prize with the other.

Wristwatch score: Axel 2, zombies 0.

Grover halted for a moment and glanced, almost knowingly, from my watch to me and then to his bare wrist.

"You need a hand moisturizer, player," I said and dropped his withered arm.

Then, I realized that if I wanted to keep the watch, I couldn't have him making false claims about missing merchandise, or allow him to go through my lost and found box. So I quickly jammed his flimsy, paper-thin arms out through the hole. It was important to put an end to this case before he filed a claim against me.

When his head popped into view once more, I mockingly held up my treasure and swung it in front of his repulsive face.

"Guess what, crack baby? I'm keeping this until I get my MP3 player back."

I knew he didn't have it, of course, but I needed an escape goat and he irritated me. Plus, I figured he'd get the word out, and pretty soon the information would start rolling in. I brazenly pocketed my new timepiece right in front of his dopey face and smirked at him.

"Go away now," I said patiently. "It's late. Walk away in shame." But, bullheadedly, he tried to come back through one more time. "You are one clingy son of a bitch! You just earned a torpedo death bomb!"

Ma, who had been standing there sleeping, suddenly opened her eyes, saw what was coming, and gave me room. I wound up and rocket-punched Grover so hard his nose exploded, spraying red and black and green into the air, and he squealed and flew backward until he crashed to the ground with a *whump!* I poked my head outside, flipped him off, and slid the window down, locking it tight. Peering through the dirty glass into the darkness for one last look, I could barely make him out, sitting there dazed and watching me.

"Are you happy? Now you're in time-out," I chastised him through the window.

Then, I squinted real hard because I thought I saw . . . I pressed against the glass and stared at . . . *zombie hair flipping me off?* Son of a bitch!

I had to be certain, so I focused harder. I still couldn't quite tell. Consequently, I angrily flipped off his hair just to make sure. I don't need no zombie going around telling everybody he got the best of me.

Ma gave me a small, tired grin and shuffled back to her room.

Feeling annoyed, I pulled down the shade and decided not to think about it anymore. After washing up, I remembered the floor and looked down. Along with the zombie sludge, there were probably thirty-two thousand gooey BBs blanketing the cracked, ancient linoleum. With a tired sigh, I figured that mess could wait until tomorrow, and I switched off the light and plodded off to bed.

Before long, I was happily dreaming I was downtown buying a new shirt. When I got to the store, they had this long table set up on the sidewalk for Crazy Days that had all kinds of clothes for sale piled on it. Then, right there, going through all the shirts and stuff, were these identical twin girls, and there were like, eight of them. It was amazing. I'm telling you, I'd never seen that many twins before, so I asked them when they were born. But they all had different birthdays, so I don't know how they pulled that off.

I went inside the store, but it wasn't a store at all. It turned out to be this hazy, colorful carnival shooting gallery. When I looked down and saw that I was holding a gun, I started peppering measle-beaked ducks on the wing. Halfway through, they were suddenly replaced by stupid zombie faces wearing toilet plunger hats, and I shot so many I won a stuffed raccoon sporting a cheesy comb-over, which I gave to Zenobia.

Best dream ever.

10
AKS AX

These days, everybody knows what's best for you, and luckily, they're eager to share. They go around saying helpful stuff that you want to hear, like how you can avoid trouble with a zombie simply by not looking him directly in the eye. Well, that old wives' tale was proven untrue just last week when I made eye contact with this well-dressed zombie before slapping off his glasses and punching him in the throat. The moral to that story is don't believe anything you hear.

Listen, the only thing you really need to know is this: live well and work hard, but not so hard that you're not well enough to keep working hard. And never be intimidated by a bespectacled zombie in a $1900 Armani.

Last summer I worked harder than ever, but I didn't mind. Plus, it wasn't all work. One day in June while he was awaiting trial, Dad came up with a major idea, which was to have a radio call-in show. Right away, I was all in because it sounded like fun. Ma thought it would be a good way to inform the public about the zombies, so she put up the money, and Dad set it all up. We got some broadcasting equipment that allows us to talk to half the state, and from our electronic workstation in the living room, Dad and I can answer everybody's questions while Ma's at work. We've been doing it for quite a while now, and it's really caught on.

Don't get confused by the names, because when we're on the air, Dad mostly goes by his prison name, Jak. I go by Ax. The show is called *Aks Ax* because people call in and "aks" us questions and we answer them. Also, sometimes it gets a little out of control and we get yelled at by the FCC dudes. Here's what our first show was like:

AX: Okay, here we are, Day One. Me and Dad got the phones. We already have a call. Hey, caller, what's up?

CALLER: Yeah. Hey, Axel, I just wanna know if those zombies I heard about are real.

AX: Real what?

CALLER: Real zombies. Are they real zombies?

AX: I can't say for sure, man. I've never seen any fake ones, but I guess that's a possibility. I'm gonna hafta check. Maybe they're fake, I don't know. I'm hangin' up now. *(click)* Good call. Next caller.

CALLER: Hey, man. This is Rick Swanson.

JAK: Cool.

CALLER: Yeah. Anyway, I was wondering what's up with those drivers who drive beside you in the other lane for like, two miles, and then when they need to be in your lane at the last minute they just cut in front of you like you're not there. Are those zombies?

JAK: Yeah, probably. I hate those guys too, man. But I guess they're better than you, so you gotta get out of their way, dude. That's their street—they're important and you're not.

CALLER: Ax, is he kidding?

AX: Who?

CALLER: What?

JAK: All right, man. Thanks for the call. That's a good point. *(click)* Next call.

CALLER: Yeah, I got a problem with one of my horses. He won't run anymore, and I can't afford to have the vet come out and look him over. He's a real sweet buckskin and I don't know what to do.

AX: Is he alive?

CALLER: What do you mean?

AX: You know, is he breathing?

CALLER: Well, that's the thing. He's kinda not breathing.

AX: That's your first problem right there.

CALLER: Yeah, but you guys know what to do, right? I mean, you know about zombies and stuff, right? Is old Buck a . . . zombie horse now? I mean, he still moves around some, but not like yesterday, before . . . before he . . . can you help? (sounding desperate)

AX: Are you crying?

CALLER: No.

AX: I can hear you sniffling.

CALLER: You're supposed to be zombie experts! Can you help me or what? (panicky)

JAK: Let me jump in here, Axel. I'll take care of it. So, caller, you like horses, huh?

CALLER: Guess so, it's my job.

JAK: And men?

CALLER: What? I didn't say that.

JAK: You didn't not say that.

CALLER: I didn't not . . . what?

JAK: Listen closely now. Are you one of those pretend cowboy dudes who wears assless chaps and prances around like a little girl?

CALLER: That ain't me—I ain't like that.

JAK: Sure you are.

CALLER: I am not, dumbshit! You probably are.

AX: Do you wear cowboy boots?

CALLER: Why?

AX: Do you like those long-sleeved, chrome-buttoned, fancily embroidered cowboy shirts? And how about those colorful pink and purple silk hankies tied around your tender neck? You like those too? Are they scrumptiously soft against your delicate neck skin?

CALLER: Hey, I got some cowboy gear, but that don't make me prissy.

JAK: Are you sure? Because, yeah, that's messed up. Come on, man, I wore that shit when I was like, eight, and you sound like you're a lot older than that. Tell you what, let me look around for a precious little cowgirl dress you can wear to the hoedown on Sunday. And some sparkly lip gloss.

CALLER: I ain't a girl, dipshit!

JAK: Don't fret, now. Just give me some time, girlfriend. Be patient and I'll find you a sassy polka dot number that'll turn the head of every cowpoke in painted-on jeans. You'll be the belle of the ball.

AX: Hey, Dad, ask him about this: if those rodeo guys can't stay on that bucking horse, why don't they wear a seat belt? Those idiots are always falling off.

JAK: Yeah!

AX: The law's the law!

CALLER: You guys are dicks!

JAK: You can't judge me. *(click)* Next call.

CALLER: Hey, man, I gotta make this fast cuz I'm calling from the Pen.

JAK: Gilby? Is that you?

CALLER: Yeah, Jak. How they hanging?

JAK: Low and slow, my brother. How's stir?

CALLER: Listen, man, I need some help. My new cellie is trippin' and I don't know what to do. I think he might be one of those zombies you guys got over there.

JAK: What does he do, Gil?

CALLER: He sometimes speaks in this other language.

JAK: Can you tell me some of it? Is it Spanish?

CALLER: Uh, that might be it. I can hear it but I can't speak it. And when he's sleeping, he does this spooky moaning. It's freaky, man.

JAK: Like he's dreaming?

CALLER: Maybe, I can't tell, I'm usually asleep. Plus—and this is really weird—he don't wear no socks on his feet.

JAK: Yeah, we got a zombie around here that don't wear no socks. He don't wear no feet, either—just totters around on stumps. You'd better sleep with one eye open, Gillie.

CALLER: All right, man. It was good talking to you.

JAK: Adios, brother. How much longer you got?

CALLER: Four years, man.

JAK: Ride high, my brother. I'll be talking to ya. *(click)* Well, gang, now you know that sockless criminals are zombies. Who's next?

CALLER: This is Cooper. Yeah, I'm having some trouble at work. This dude who's worked here for half the time I have is always trying to tell me what to do. I'm close to popping him, but I don't wanna lose my job. Got any advice?

AX: Is he a zombie?

CALLER: A what?

AX: A zombie.

CALLER: He might be. How can you tell?

AX: Did you ask him?

CALLER: You mean, ask him if he's a zombie?

AX: Why would you do that?

CALLER: Huh?

JAK: Axel, I'll take this. Caller, let me tell you something. When you're in the wild, and your life is on the line, you have to look at a creature's eyes to know what you're up against. Listen, are his eyes slitted like a cat's or round like a zombie's?

CALLER: Um, they're sort of diagonal, I think.

JAK: Okay, he's poisonous.

CALLER: He's what?

JAK: Back out of there slowly—no sudden movements.

CALLER: He's in the next room, in his office.

JAK: Okay, here's what you need to do: creep in there quietly, but don't stand too close to him.

CALLER: All right, give me a sec . . . almost there . . . okay, I'm inside. He's here, sitting at his desk, but he's looking at me so I have to whisper.

JAK: How close is he?

CALLER: Two feet.

JAK: Perfect. Now listen closely. Act nonchalant, and look at your watch. That will give him the impression that you're late for an appointment with the boss. Can you do that?

CALLER: Yeah, I'm doing it now, but he's looking at me with an annoyed expression.

JAK: Does he look like a zombie?

CALLER: Um, I think so, yeah.

JAK: Okay, these next few seconds are crucial. How you feeling?

CALLER: I—I don't know. I'm okay, I guess. Just nervous. He's looking right at me.

JAK: All right, you're doing fine, kid. You can do this, we're gonna talk you through it. Now, slowly back away while looking frustrated—that'll confuse him. Also, if you have any cologne with you, now's the time to give yourself a good coating—that'll throw off his sensor. If it's cheap cologne, he'll be even less likely to get near you. Do you use cheap cologne?

CALLER: Yeah, but, I—I don't have any with me. He—he wants to know who the hell I'm talking to on the phone. I'm backing out. I'm almost to the door now.

JAK: Mister, get the hell out of there, stat!

CALLER: I'm out! I'm heading back to my office. He's yelling at me through the door . . . he's calling me a dick. Whew! That was close!

JAK: You're damn right it was—they can be very unpredictable. You did good, kid. You're lucky I was here to talk you through it.

CALLER: Wow, thanks a lot!

JAK: Hey, no problem, that's why we're here, man. Just call again if you need us. *(click)*

AX: Another job well done, Dad.

JAK: Like taking candy from an unborn baby.

AX: Who would even give candy to an unborn baby?

JAK: Do I look like the candy FBI?

AX: A little around the eyes.

JAK: Back to work. Next caller, what's your beef?

CALLER: Hey, Duncan here from Milberg.

JAK: Whatever.

AX: Milberg Mustangs? No way!

CALLER: Yeah, man. Go Mustangs! Anyway, I was listening to that last caller—how do you know if someone is a zombie or just pretending?

JAK: Pretending to be a caller?

AX: Let me take this, Dad. First of all, your average zombie ain't much of an actor, so if he's pretending, you can tell real easy—it's like giving candy to an unborn baby.

CALLER: Well, this isn't like that. I know this dude; he's just a regular guy, but he might be pretending to be a zombie. Thing is, he looks real.

AX: Listen man, you need to know this: zombie makeup is hard to come by, and when you bring it home, your mom finds where you hid it, gets suspicious and throws it away, and then she tries to ground you. But she can't ground you if it isn't yours, right?

CALLER: Uh, I don't know for sure. That sounds right, I guess.

AX: That's what I told her. But she tried to ground me anyway. What do you do when that happens?

CALLER: Well, I don't really get grounded—I'm married, so I get yelled at, I guess.

AX: Exactly. See? I hope you're listening, Ma. Thanks for supporting me, Duncan. I'll tell Ma to call you tomorrow so you can explain it to her.

CALLER: Ah, no, don't do that. So, do you know how to tell the difference between, you know, the phonies and the real zombies?

AX: I can see you're not the kind of guy who gives up. I like that.

CALLER: Right, so this dude looks like a zombie, but he seems so real. Do you think he's faking?

AX: Does he wear sensible shoes?

CALLER: Jeez, ah, I think so.

AX: There ya go.

CALLER: He's a zombie?

AX: He sounds like a tool.

CALLER: Maybe he is a zombie, I wish I knew . . .

JAK: Hey, Axel, let me jump in here. Caller, you sound like a good boy who's just made a bad decision, that's all. You know better than to be hassling your friend about his shoes.

CALLER: Um, okay. Wait, what? I'm not hassling anyone. And I'm no boy. I'm a man.

JAK: Sure you are. Now listen, you need us as much as we need you. Don't be too hard on yourself, and remember, we're here to help you. It's important to stay calm, boy.

CALLER: I just want some zombie advice. And I'm not a boy.

JAK: Sure you are. Now, stop beating yourself up. Just relax and use your boyish charm to win over this zombie poser.

CALLER: What is wrong with you?

JAK: It's okay, you're just a little nervous and you're blaming yourself. It happens to every lady-boy now and then.

CALLER: *Boy?* Who you calling *boy?* (fuming)

JAK: I wasn't really paying attention, but I'm pretty sure it was you. Listen, it's okay, boy-o. You don't have to prove your manhood to me.

CALLER: *You* listen! I'm thirty-nine, *boy!*

AX: You're a thirty-nine-year-old boy? That's weird. Does your ma dress you for school in the morning?

JAK: Yeah, caller, that really ain't something you should be bragging about.

CALLER: I'm gonna come down there and pull your eyeballs out!

AX: Do you do teeth? Cuz I got a bad molar way in the back.

JAK: You need to get a girlfriend, dude. Then you'd calm down and stay on task, and be more of a team player. *(click)* Next call.

CALLER: Hey, Ax, first time caller, man. I love your show, eh? I'm calling from Montreal, and I got a problem with my landlord, eh? He's threatening to evict me cuz I got a little turtle in a cage and he says pets aren't allowed. But come on, it's a turtle in a cage, eh? What do you think I should do?

AX: Is it a zombie turtle? I heard those are illegal in Montana.

CALLER: I'm in Canada, man. Montreal.

AX: You're from Montreal? That reminds me, I went to Canada once.

CALLER: You did?

AX: Well, practically—I was at the border.

CALLER: That's pretty close, eh?

AX: The thing is, I never actually made it to the border cuz my boss wouldn't let me off work that day. But I was gonna watch this wildlife show about Canada once. And yesterday I read my lacrosse magazine from cover to cover without stopping once—and I'm not making that up.

JAK: You did that? Yesterday? You're a good reader, son.

AX: Thanks, Dad. And thanks, caller. Good job on that Montana thing. *(click)* Now, back to the phones.

CALLER: Hey, Axel, it's me. I was listening to your stupid show. When you gonna grow up?

AX: Hey! Lisa, is that you? It's good to hear from you, it's been so long.

CALLER: You been thinking about me?

AX: I have to tell you something. In junior high, when we were dating, you meant everything to me. I thought about you all the time.

CALLER: Aw, that's nice. What about now?

AX: When you bailed, I wondered where I went wrong. And as I missed you and thought about you a lot, I got this really strong feeling for you.

CALLER: Love?

AX: No, it's that other thing.

CALLER: Affection?

AX: No, it was more like, whaddyacall . . . disgust. What the hell was I thinking? You know I never did drugs, Lisa, but tell me, was I somehow on crack back then? Did you put me on crack when I wasn't watching?

CALLER: You're a horse's ass!

AX: Oh, no you don't—I'm not looking for a psycho girlfriend, but thanks for asking. I wouldn't touch you with a ten-foot zombie. Stay sweet! *(click)* Okay, another great call— it's good to get in touch with old friends again, ain't it?

"Hey, Dad, where you been?"

"Ax, I heard some of that last call when I was out in the back. Who was that last caller?"

"I was wondering where you went."

"I wasn't fighting."

"Okay, I didn't say you were, but . . . were you fighting again?"

"Come on, man. Who just called?"

"I don't know, dude. She wanted your number, though."

"Really?"

"No. Who's next?"

"It's probably some stupid-ass needing a beating."

"Come on, Dad. Let's be peaceful."

"Just doing my job."

"Make an effort. All right, caller, whaddya got for us?"

CALLER: Hi, this is Preston Johansson. Axel, I'm having a problem with your dad. He was just out in the alley threatening me and my son with a sledgehammer. What's his deal, anyway?

AX: Is this a zombie monkey calling? Wait a minute, I know who this is. Ashby, you hairy little rascal, is that you? How did you dial the phone? Are you out of your monkey cage again? I'm gonna paddle your hairy ass, you naughty little monkey.

CALLER: Are you a jagoff?

AX: Hold on—let me check with Ma. Hang on.

CALLER: Do you always have to check with your ma?

AX: Good question. I'll go check.

CALLER: You probably like making it with zombies.

AX: Shut up, bed-wetter!

CALLER: What did you call me?!

AX: What? Oh, I wasn't talking to you. It's my dad—he's making a face and whispering stuff.

CALLER: What did he say? Was it about me?

AX: Shut your spit hole, zombie jockey!

CALLER: *What?!*

AX: Not you—my dad. Let me ask you something. If you were a zombie, and I knew it but you didn't, would you want me to tell you?

CALLER: Um, I don't know . . . I guess so, right?

AX: What? Oh, not you. I was talking to my—*I'm about to go Randy Marsh on your ass!*

CALLER: What the hell! Are you talking to me?!

AX: Huh? I'm gonna slap the stupid right off your face!

CALLER: You're not talking to me, are you?

AX: What? My dad's a dick. I'll hammer-slap you with enough force to turn off the stars!

CALLER: You'd better not be talking to me.

AX: Hey, thumb-sucker, I'm not the one on everybody's hate radar.

CALLER: All right, man, if you're gonna argue with your dad all day you should get off the phone and keep it private.

AX: Dad's in the alley taking a wiz.

CALLER: *You son of a—*

AX: Hey, Ashby, great news. Ma says you can stay out and play a little longer. Just don't get into Mr. Burke's garbage cans again, you little scrote-monkey. Last time, you left a ton of your used-up underpants scattered all over his yard.

CALLER: I'm gonna scatter you!

AX: *¡Cuídate, cabrón!*—Beware, you bastard!

CALLER: What did you call me?

AX: That's the spirit! Now, tell you what I'm gonna do, Preston. I'm sending you a copy of my new CD called *Eat It, Biz-ee-otch! (click)* All right, next caller.

CALLER: Hi, Axel. First time caller—love your show. You gotta tell me more about the zombies. Can they like, go to other people's houses, or just yours? Because I'll be honest, I'm a little concerned, man.

AX: Caller, you have a funny voice. Are you a monkey?

CALLER: What?

AX: Is this a monkey calling? Are you holding the phone with your tail?

CALLER: Why would I do that?

AX: What else are you going to use your tail for?

CALLER: I don't have a tail—I'm not a monkey!

AX: Are you sure?

CALLER: Yeah!

AX: *Are* you?

CALLER: I think I would know!

AX: *Would* you? Maybe you don't know that you're a monkey.

JAK: I don't think they do, Ax. He doesn't know.

AX: Good point, Dad. *(click)* Okay, good call. Who's next— and it better not be another monkey.

CALLER: Yeah, I'm starting to get tired of my wife's constant whining and complaining. Nearly every damn day this week it's been something different. Monday it was, "My sister is dying!" Then it was, "My father has cancer!" Yesterday it was, "Make your own pork chops." It doesn't stop. As it is, every day at work is a crappy day for me, and then I gotta come home and listen to that depressing shit. She needs to get over it already. It's pissing me off.

JAK: Okay, that's a good question. You've got issues, asscrack.

CALLER: What did you call me?

JAK: You're welcome. Now listen, here's what we're going to do. We're going to have a lesson in sympathy.

CALLER: What? I don't need a damn lesson!

JAK: I think you do. Here's how it works. I kick your ass, then we'll see if I feel sorry for you.

CALLER: Who the hell do you think you're talking to?!

JAK: Oh, wait—don't tell me. I love guessing games. Now let me guess . . . Marla? Is this my ex-wife, Marla? How did you get this number? And what about the restraining order?

CALLER: I'm coming down there, man!

JAK: That's a good idea. I've still got a chalk outline on the driveway from the last dude. Let's see if we can get a match. How tall are you?

AX: Good question, Dad. *(click)* Okay, let's get to the next caller.

CALLER: Hello? Hi, I don't know if you can help me. My name is Denton and I work as a cashier at the supermarket. I had to unplug my home computer because my manager was hacking my files in an attempt to learn my secret identity. I just know he's a zombie spy.

JAK: Don't worry; you're being taken care of now.

CALLER: Really? I can't tell you what that means to me. Last week when I found out my landlady was a zombie alien, she tried to brainwash me through the pipes.

JAK: Okay, I've just uploaded the proper software. You are now my cyber puppet and I control you completely, so go ahead and plug your computer back in.

CALLER: Do I have to?

JAK: I'm controlling you as we speak.

CALLER: Yes, sir. (meekly)

AX: Done and done. *(click)* Next caller.

CALLER: I need help.

AX: What's the story, man?

CALLER: I refuse to live with zombies. I did it once back in the sixties, and I ain't gonna do it again.

AX: Dad, this one's for you.

JAK: Grandma? Is that you?

CALLER: *Grandma?* Hey, jackass, you wanna know what it's like to be a corpse?!

JAK: I wanna know what it's like to eat a whole birthday cake—is that the same thing? Never mind. Listen, I'll tell you what I'll do. I know it's not Christmas yet, but I'm going to give you a sweet discount on a cozy little holiday ass beating. *¿Acaso quieres que te dé una paliza hasta el borde de la muerte?*—Shall I beat you to within an inch of your life?

CALLER: Like you could! And how would that help me?

JAK: Why does it always have to be about you?

AX: You can't unsing that song, Dad. Good save. No need to apologize, caller. *(click)* Okay, who's on the line now?

CALLER: Hey, Ax. This is Bert, from Bert's Trucking. Put Jak on. I'd like a crack at that dude.

AX: What? You'd like his crack?

CALLER: I didn't say that!

AX: You're gay for Jak? Oh man, I can't deal. This reminds me of the time I cut off a zombie's hand and he punched me with the stump! Come on, man. That is not what this show is about. I'm gonna hang up now—stay away from the model airplane glue, people. *(click)* Come on, callers—no more weird shit, okay? Dad, why don't you take this next one? God!

JAK: It's covered—and don't be so hard on that last guy, son. There are a lot of women out there who want me—I guess we should have expected some spillover. Hello, caller, what's your zombie situation?

CALLER: Ah, I just need some help with my car.

JAK: Is it a zombie?

CALLER: I don't even know how to answer that.

JAK: You just put the phone up next to your mouth and say your answer. That's okay, take your time. We have to be sure.

CALLER: Okay. Um, no, it's not a zombie. It's a car.

JAK: There's your problem right there. If it were a zombie, you wouldn't be having all these issues; zombies are virtually maintenance-free. You can't do any better than that, my friend. No maintenance. You really should think about it.

CALLER: Okay, um, I will. What about my car?

JAK: What about it?

CALLER: It just clicks and don't start.

JAK: Have you checked the zombie fluid?

CALLER: What? My fwend told me you could help.

JAK: Did you just say "fwend"?

CALLER: . . . no . . .

JAK: You did so!

CALLER: I did not! You didn't hear me wight.

JAK: There! You did it again! You talk like a baby!

AX: I'm gonna stop this right here. *(click)* Okay, we got that taken care of. Let's take the next call—wait, I've got an important announcement, listeners. We've just received a notice from one of our sponsors that the show is getting a little too violent. Yeah, this is our first day, and Dad's already been in three fights—and we've been on the air for less than an hour. So, let's everybody just calm down, and by everybody I mean Dad. Are you listening?

"I heard you," Dad murmurs.

"Dad?" I'm feeling suspicious. "Where ya been?"

"Nowhere."

"Were you fighting again?"

"No." He looks suspicious.

"Then how come your shirt is torn?"

"How come it's not?" He slides his hand up to cover the ripped-off pocket. That's really suspicious.

"What?"

"Yours is," Dad says, trying to blame me again.

"Did you hear my important announcement?"

"What announcement?" He blinks a few times. "Yeah, I heard it."

"Good. Next caller. You worried about the zombies too?"

CALLER: Ah, sure. Um, anyway, I'm having trouble with my Harley. I don't know if you can help or not.

AX: I know that voice. Is this that dude with the Harley?

CALLER: Yeah, man, that's me! How'd you know?

AX: I recognized your voice.

CALLER: All right, man!

AX: So how's it going, dude?

CALLER: It's going great, man. Except my old lady kicked me out. Then she had some dudes come and take my bike, man. My Harley's gone, dude.

AX: Oh man, that ain't right. You need your wheels.

CALLER: Heard that, bro.

AX: Got any new ink?

CALLER: Yeah, I got this cool tat of my old lady on a hog and she's got angel wings and a halo.

AX: That sounds righteous, man. Thanks for calling, bro.

CALLER: Right on. Lay low.

AX: Far out. *(click)* That was that dude with the Harley; I know that dude. Okay, maybe I know this caller too. Hey, man, what's going on? Do I know you?

CALLER: No, this is Byron Crantz. Do you ever have trouble with pants?

AX: Lately, yeah—a lot of trouble.

CALLER: I hear pants calling me.

AX: They call you?

CALLER: It's when I'm in bed late at night, you know?

AX: What happens?

CALLER: I hear 'em in my closet, calling me . . . mocking me.

AX: Mocking pants, huh? Well, this one time I couldn't get these pants off. They were really cool, and I was tugging and tugging, but it was like they were not gonna come off, and now that I think about it, I bet they were mocking me—they refused to cooperate.

CALLER: Are they still on?

AX: No. Here's what I did: first, I wrenched off the right boot, then the left boot.

CALLER: Did you get the pants off then?

AX: Yeah, after that it only took me like, two seconds to yank those bad boys off.

CALLER: Pants can be a bitch.

AX: No deuce! Next time I go after a zombie's black cargos, I'm bringing help . . . or a crowbar. Oh, and P.S., if you take his killer boots off first, the pants usually slide right off. *(click)* Great question. Next caller.

CALLER: I got this thing, like a sharp pain in my forehead.

AX: Is it a zombie bite? How does it feel?

CALLER: Like a migraine, maybe.

AX: Have you always had zombie migraines?

CALLER: What? No, I don't think so.

AX: Is it a brain tumor?

CALLER: Shit, I hope not.

AX: How long have you been a neurosurgeon?

CALLER: I'm not.

AX: Then how come you know so much about cancerous brain tumors?

CALLER: I don't, and neither do you.

AX: Let me be the judge of that. Now, just how big is this tumor?

CALLER: It's not a tumor! It's just an ongoing pain.

AX: How long have you had it?

CALLER: About three weeks now.

AX: Taken any aspirin?

CALLER: What do you think? It hurts like hell.

AX: You've been to hell? Dude, what's that like?

CALLER: How stupid are you?

AX: Well, I'm not the one stupid enough to get a brain tumor. Do you see me calling you and complaining about a brain tumor?

JAK: Hold on, Ax. Caller, have you been stabbed?

CALLER: What? No, it's inside, like behind my eyes. I tried everything and nothing helps relieve it.

JAK: Is it an old stab wound? Like, from a vengeful zombie?

CALLER: No.

JAK: Does it hurt?

CALLER: Yeah, all the time.

AX: Like a brain tumor?

JAK: Or an old stab wound?

CALLER: What the—

JAK: That sucks, man. Let us know how it turns out. And take an aspirin.

CALLER: But—

JAK: You gotta get those stab wounds treated, folks. *(click)*

AX: You don't have to tell me twice. Also, you should feel around real good to find that damn tumor, then remove it—that's one way to remove a tumor, and that alone could save your life right there.

JAK: It could be a stabbing tumor.

AX: I've heard of those.

JAK: They had a bunch of 'em in Ghana.

AX: Ghana? Is that where they have all those trees?

JAK: They got more trees than people there, probably.

AX: So the trees could run the country?

JAK: I bet.

AX: Cool. Hey, does everybody get to live in a wicked tree house?

JAK: I would.

AX: And that's how they get the stabbing tumors? From the trees?

JAK: Wouldn't surprise me at all.

AX: How'd you learn all that stuff?

JAK: I saw it on a thing once.

AX: Yeah, I think I saw that one too. Isn't that where they have those mondo snakes that eat hippos and lions and bananas?

JAK: Damn right. That's why I'm not Ghana go there.

AX: Good one, Dad!

JAK: No shit!

AX: Score!

JAK: All right, just remember, callers, get your stab wounds checked out.

AX: And your tumors.

JAK: They can hurt like a royal bitch. Just ask that last guy.

AX: He had the courage *de la mozzarella*—of mozzarella.

JAK: And the quickness *de un iguana*—of a lizard.

AX: Okay, let's take the next call.

CALLER: Hey, man. What kind of call-in show is this? We got serious questions about the zombie takeover and shit, but you idiot cobnockers don't help anybody.

JAK: I could help you.

CALLER: How *you* gonna help *me?*

JAK: I'm gonna help you with your girlfriend situation.

CALLER: What do you know about it?

JAK: Here's the deal, Spanky. I sense you're a little tense about this latest bout of zombie activity. So to make you feel better, I'll come over and give you a good monkey thumpin', then take your girlfriend to the movies. What kind of movies does she like?

CALLER: I'm gonna kill you! Hey, wait a minute—aren't you the dude who owes me $200?

JAK: No, that's that other guy. And no need to thank me, man. It's, uh, what is it called, that . . . *public service*—yeah, that's it. It's a public service, dude. No charge, I'm just glad to help out. *(click)* Okay, who's the next caller?

CALLER: Hey, you gotta help me! I'm having trouble in my neighborhood. This grungy-ass gang keeps terrorizing my kid sister and her friends and everybody. I've never seen 'em around here before. They could be zombies, I don't know. They got like, weird clothes and eyes and shit.

AX: Are they there now?

CALLER: Yeah, man, they're hasslin' an old dude in the street!

AX: How many?

CALLER: Ah, it looks like maybe ten or twelve. They're all raggedy and shit, and they look drunk or something. They're in the street right now and they got him surrounded, man!

AX: We're rolling in five. What's your address, dude?

CALLER: Six eleven Elm Street—it's behind The Pizza Krust.

AX: I know where that is. *(click)* Let's book, Dad!

-OFF THE AIR-

-FORTY-THREE MINUTES LATER-

AX: Okay, listeners, we're back. Sorry it took so long. That was serious zombie madness over there, bro. We went to Warren's neighborhood where there were like, a dozen smelly jacktools wandering around and pestering this old dude for a meal—like trying to bite him and shit. But they ain't no more, eh, Dad?

JAK: Not unless they use their hair—everything else is broken. Good news, hey: I wrangled an easy $200 out of this rotting tuxedo dude with one arm and two legs. It was like taking a wallet from a baby. Also, quick shout-out to Rusty and Mr. Abrams over there for helping us out—thanks for leaving in the middle of your *Asteroids* game just to pitch in, man. I know how hard that is, I've been in that position before. And Warren, call us again if any more knuckle-nuts show up and need to be ironed out, my brother.

AX: All right, let's take some more calls.

CALLER: Axel, this is Ma.

AX: Ma who?

MA: Listen, spankmonkey, the only reason I decided to sponsor you two idiots and your stupid call-in radio show was you agreed to cut those weeds and take care of that raccoon problem, remember? Is it done?

AX: Hey, wait a minute. Who is this? Your voice sounds familiar . . .

JAK: Is this a zombie ventriloquist on a stolen cell phone?

AX: Sorry, but we don't have any raccoons for sale. Thanks anyway.

JAK: Yeah, and if you really are a zombie ventriloquist, what do you want with one of our raccoons?

AX: Are you gonna eat it?

JAK: You're gonna eat a raccoon?

AX: Ugh! You're probably gonna eat it raw. You're a zombie, that's what you do. Gross!

JAK: Why can't you cook your raccoon like everybody else?

AX: What's wrong with you?

JAK: You're not eating one of our raccoons!

AX: And how do we know you're a real zombie ventriloquist?

JAK: Do you have two forms of ID?

AX: Why should we believe you in the first place?

JAK: What have you ever done for us?

MA: *Hey!* Are you two dork slaps done?

AX: Well, I guess I could check with Ma, but she's kinda partial towards the raccoons. They're like her special little pets.

JAK: She even has names for 'em.

AX: Yeah, she calls them all "Bastard." She probably named them out of love.

JAK: So don't hold your breath, but we'll bring it up at the next family card game and get back to you. In the meantime, attention all raccoons: if you can hear this, you need to run and hide. Repeat: run and hide.

AX: Caller, do you know where Ma is? I'm getting hungry and we're out of pizza.

JAK: Hey, zombie ventriloquist, have you got any pizza?

MA: I can wait all day, shizzheads!

JAK: Dor? Is that you? Sorry I didn't return your call last night, but it was Friday and I was at the club . . . stripping.

MA: Right, that happens. (sarcastic)

AX: Ma? Is that you? Hey, thanks for checking in. Are you calling for our pizza order?

MA: One of you better grow up and take some responsibility!

AX: Right on. *(click)* Okay, that was probably just another wrong number.

JAK: That was weird, son. She seemed to know our names.

AX: Yeah, scary. Let's take a real call now.

JAK: You know your ma is gonna kill you for hanging up on her, right?

AX: I wasn't even here when that happened.

JAK: Right on. Me neither—that was some other guys.

AX: Okay then, let's take this caller. Hey, man, what's up?

CALLER: Hey, Axel, is that Jak there really named Juan Anderson?

AX: That's his fugitive name. What's up?

CALLER: I know that crackwhacker. I thought I killed him, that's what's up.

JAK: Aunt Daisy, is that you?

CALLER: Juan friggin' Anderson! I'm gonna dip you in the mop bucket and clean the floor with you!

JAK: Auntie, your voice changed. Have you been smoking crack in the potato cellar again?

CALLER: Shut up with the "auntie" crap. Get ready cuz I'm coming to beat your ass good.

JAK: Wait. How good? Cuz if it's gonna be just a mediocre ass beating, I can't say I'm all in. But call back when you've upped your game. Remember, strive to be the best.

CALLER: No, it's gonna be a real good ass whuppin', jerkweed.

JAK: Okay, let me see if I got this right. You want *me* . . . to come down *there* . . . and beat your ass? Jeez, I don't know. I'm really kinda busy. Can we do it some other time?

CALLER: Listen, nobody's beating my ass, got it?

JAK: Why? What makes your ass so special? Or, is that it? Are you special ed? Hey, man, I'm sorry—I didn't know.

CALLER: I'm not special ed! You are, but that's not why I'm calling.

JAK: I can hook you up with an agency that helps your kind.

CALLER: My *kind?*

JAK: It's cool, man. Don't worry, your ass will be in good hands, Ed—can I call you Ed?

CALLER: I'm gonna beat your ass!

JAK: You want to beat my ass? Well, I won't lie to you—I'm overdue for a good ass beating. But, the thing is, my schedule is pretty full. How about if I call you when I have an opening?

CALLER: You owe me, Juan Anderson!

JAK: Hey, I owe a lot of things. What do I owe you?

CALLER: Try two hundred bucks.

JAK: Sounds kinda steep, but what the hell. You're the one with the money.

CALLER: I'm getting my dough. How do you wanna do it?

JAK: Hmm, what are the choices?

CALLER: I come down there and beat it out of you.

JAK: You'll need a second appointment for that.

CALLER: Appointment? I need an appointment to tear your head off?

JAK: You do if you're gonna pay me back the two hundred bucks.

CALLER: I don't owe you nothin'!

JAK: Fine. We'll call it even, then.

AX: Good save, Dad. *(click)* We're gonna hafta get a secretary to take this kind of information down, like appointments and ass beatings and stuff, you know? All right, that was a good call. Let's take another one.

CALLER: Hey, guys, I'm having trouble sleeping at night. I've tried everything, but nothing works and I'm starting to freak out a little. I think it's the zombies that are worrying me.

JAK: Have you tried sleeping pills?

CALLER: Yeah, I've tried everything.

JAK: Have you tried warm milk before you hit the sack?

CALLER: Yeah, yeah. I think I must have tried just about every remedy there is.

JAK: Have you tried counting sheep?

CALLER: I've tried everything.

JAK: Have you tried counting zombies?

CALLER: No.

JAK: How about soft music, like meditation music?

CALLER: How do you count music? Are you even listening, man? I've tried all that stuff. None of it works.

AX: (mumbling) Have you tried kicking your own ass?

CALLER: What was that?

AX: Huh?

JAK: Caller, are you tired?

CALLER: Dude, I've slept like, maybe three hours the last four nights.

JAK: Have you tried reading a book before bedtime?

CALLER: Come on, man. Can you help me or what?

JAK: All right, I've got an idea. Let's play word association. I say a word and you say whatever pops into your mind. Ready?

CALLER: Sure.

JAK: Okay, here we go: Me

CALLER: I

JAK: Are

CALLER: Am

JAK: Daddy's

CALLER: Momma's

JAK: Girl

CALLER: Boy

JAK: Ax, did you hear that? Hey, caller, you're a momma's boy. What's that like?

CALLER: What? I didn't say that!

JAK: Yes, you did. But don't worry, you're just feeling the

shame that results from being away from your momma too long.

AX: Nice work, Dad. Caller, aren't you glad you called now? That's free psychotherapy, man. You should feel better after the shame goes away.

CALLER: What the hell? I ain't some little kid who needs to be coddled!

JAK: Hell's bells, dude. Now you want me to coddle you? I'll tell you what, I may be a lot of things, but I'm a pretty good coddler.

CALLER: You're out of your mind! You ain't touching me.

AX: He's probably gay for zombie chicks, Dad. Is that it, caller? And you're just too ashamed to tell anyone? It's all right, dude, don't be proud. Just admitting it like you did takes courage. We're glad we could be here for you.

CALLER: You guys suck!

JAK: Oh man. *(click)* Did you hear that? He was attracted to girl zombies, and now he's not anymore. He has so much shame.

AX: Good job, Dad. Next caller, are you having trouble sleeping with zombie chicks?

CALLER: Hey, Axel and Mr. Jak. Um, no, I'm actually having trouble with my hard drive and I don't know what to do.

JAK: Hard drive? You wanna know a hard drive? That's when you're dodgin' the scales cuz you're over the limit by thirty-five hundred and you're avoiding the state troopers as you're smokin' through the Arkansas toolies thirty mph over the speed limit in your 18-wheeler on dirt roads nine feet wide and the woods are so close they're jumping through your windows and it's three in the morning and a renegade squirrel hops in the cab and gnaws at your nuts and you toss him out the window and you haven't slept for two days and you're so wired on caffeine you can hear your fingernails growing. That's a hard drive, my friend!

CALLER: Um . . . okay . . . thanks.

AX: Right on, Dad. Good advice—another zombie problem solved. Thanks, caller. *(click)* Let's take another one.

CALLER: Sorry if de English is bad or de gramma not best. I not from a country using dis languages.

JAK: You said it, man. Why do you think the Pilgrims wrote the Constitution in the first place?

CALLER: What? De comstinution . . . what?

JAK: That's right, man. You and Sam Hancock and those other dudes.

CALLER: You bin in hepping de peoples wif de problems, no?

JAK: That's why we're here, my friend. Lay it on me.

CALLER: I be calling for you to hep me, okay? You do dat?

JAK: Tell you what, I'll do better than that. I'll help you out real good. What's your problem, chief?

CALLER: You dudies hep me wit me zommie problem?

AX: Dad, did he call us dudies?

JAK: Yeah, we're dudies. Sure, we'll help you, caller. Give us the story on your zombie problem, brother.

CALLER: Dat is being beddy good. Beddy good!

JAK: We're here to help, ace.

CALLER: Dis zommie mans what I needed to be killed; dis zommie mans he call de names being bad and knock me down.

JAK: Sounds like you've got a zombie bully problem, partner. Those are my favorite people, cuz I get to beat their bad asses and hear the applause.

CALLER: Beating de asses can do? His asses am being beddy beddy bad.

JAK: If this guy has a very bad ass, then we can fix it. Tell me, is this zombie bully living in your yard?

CALLER: Hims in yard and me thinking I am be killing hims to det, dat's what now.

JAK: Hold on there, cowboy. Don't go killing him to death— leave that for the professionals.

CALLER: You be beddy good mans, beddy good mans.

JAK: I know that. Now listen, here's what I want you to do: sit down and help yourself to a nice big piece of rhubarb pie.

CALLER: How am I be eating de pies and he be knocking me down wit de beddy, beddy bad asses? I must be doing de killing on hims.

JAK: No, no, no. That's your inner voice. Do not listen to your inner voice. Do you hear me?

CALLER: De inna voice say KILL! KILL! KILL!

JAK: Do you have an outer voice? One that says, "Send in the ninjas"?

CALLER: De outta voice say KILL! KILL! KILL ON HIMS!

JAK: Okay, no more listening to your inner voice or your outer voice. From now on, you listen only to your third voice: me. Got it?

CALLER: You beddy good mans. I be doing de killing on de bully zommie mans now. You gibbing de good adbice.

JAK: Okay, try to stay in the circle, Gumby. It sounds like you're all hopped up on sugar donuts. First, I need you to put down the donuts. Can you do that for me?

CALLER: I am not knowing dese Gumby nuts.

JAK: Pay attention now! I had a problem like yours once and I took care of it. Here's what I did. I waited for the right time and jumped the bully. Then the next day I chased his friends down and beat them too. But does that make me a hero? You bet your ass it does.

CALLER: So I am be jumping on de bully mans now?

JAK: Are you bastard-mad enough to do it?

CALLER: De bastard is de . . . who is bastard?

JAK: No! Are you bastard-*mad?* You gotta be a mean son of a bitch if you're gonna rumble, son!

CALLER: I now be killing on you for calling me de son for bitch and bastard! I come dere to be killing on you. You hab de beddy, beddy bad asses.

JAK: You really need to be killing on someone, don't you? I used to be like that.

AX: You still are, Dad.

JAK: I know.

AX: And you're getting worse.

JAK: That's enough!

AX: Okay, well done. That was a long call. *(click)* Who do we have on the line now?

CALLER: This is Gordon. I got a solution for the zombie dilemma.

AX: Trent, is that you?

CALLER: What? No, this is Gordon—Gordon Wilson.

AX: Trent, I recognize your voice, man. *You're Trent Erickson!*

CALLER: Shut up! I am not! I just moved here. I called to give you some advice about those green dudes stumbling around. We had the same situation in . . . another state—not Idaho.

AX: Trent, man, I thought you were in the Witness Protection Program somewhere in Idaho.

CALLER: I am. I mean, I'm not in Idaho; I'm here. And I'm not Trent!

AX: All right, man. It's good to hear from you again. I'm glad you're back in town.

CALLER: *Dammit, Axel! (click)*

AX: Cool! That was one of my old buds, Trent Erickson. I'm gonna hafta look up that dickslapper now that he's back. Plus, he had some good advice for the zombie invasion. Thanks, Trent. I'll tell Bianca Jensen you're back, she'll be glad to hear it. I won't tell those bikers though. Okay, next caller.

CALLER: Hi, guys. My crap job sucks monkey nads.

AX: You need my three-step plan. First, stop sucking monkey nads. Second, how much does that earn? Third, that's sick.

CALLER: So you're a funny guy? Should I tell you I have trained killer moths at my disposal?

AX: All right, man, calm down. I'm here to help. I was trying to tell you to take that civil surface exam, and then you can work for the post office or the federal government.

CALLER: I don't know, man. I hate tests. Is there any other way? You know, like, a way around all the bureaucracy?

AX: Yeah, you can take some training at the community college.

CALLER: That sounds pretty cool. Is that all there is to it?

AX: That's all there is, man. And after you finish the training, you just take the civil surface exam.

CALLER: All right. I'll do that, then. Thanks, Ax.

AX: Right on, brother. Good luck. *(click)* Next caller.

CALLER: Yeah, ah, I've been listenin' to this show all day, and I got a problem.

JAK: Let me guess: you got into your grandmother's liquor cabinet and now you need an ass beating?

CALLER: That's my problem, right there. You dickwads think you're so tough. I'll take you both right now!

AX: Hey, I don't do blind dates, man.

CALLER: I'll pull your arms off!

JAK: You'd better take your heart medication, old man, then find a good hiding place, because a good old-fashioned nut choking is about to be delivered to your damn house.

CALLER: Old man? This *old man* is twenty-four!

AX: You've had twenty-four old men? Well, did you hear that, everybody? That's the mark to beat, fellas.

JAK: That's setting the bar pretty high, dude. *(click)* Did you hear what he said? That old guy has a heart problem and he's a male prostitute for the aged. No wonder he called in—he just likes to brag. Glad we could help. That's why we're here, folks. Next caller.

CALLER: Yo yo yo. Dis is Lil Ditty. I gots to know 'bout dem zizzos shamblin' around and whatnot. I don't need none a dat shit goin' down 'round my crib.

JAK: Zizzos? Wait a minute—is this Little Shitty, the rapper?

CALLER: Yo, I gots rhymes, diggity dog.

JAK: Can you read my mind?

CALLER: Hey, yo, don't be talkin' 'bout reading no minds, homes.

JAK: Right on, my brother. What am I thinking now?

CALLER: You thinkin' what's it like to be poppin' like Lil Ditty.

JAK: Okay, but did you get the other thing I was thinking?

CALLER: Yo, what other thing?

JAK: I was thinking how funny it would be to send two of my zombie bouncers over to your baby crib to thrash your wimpy, obnoxious ass. Do you wear an assdiaper in your baby crib? Is your assdiaper blinged out? Do you have a blinged-out baby bottle filled with milk? That you drink in your baby crib? While you wear a blinged-out assdiaper? Shizzle fizzle delizzle mizzle?

CALLER: What? Don't be hatin' a playuh cuz a his swagger.

AX: No, really—Dad's right. You gots to gets yo ass beat, Snoop. It's the right call. We'll get a couple of our best zombie tough guys to catch up with you at your baby crib.

CALLER: You trippin'.

JAK: Here's the deal, Ice Pee: first, I need your email address so I can send you my special "I bust rhymes because I'm

talentless so somebody needs to turbo-spank my useless ass"
virus.

CALLER: Y'all gonna get *yo* ass whipped, Clyde!

JAK: The next thing I'll need is for you to tell your mother to
quit calling me. Sure, she's hot and all, but I've got enough fine
ladies. Now, don't talk to me anymore unless you want the
Jakhammer rollin' down your tracks. *(click)* Okay, don't nobody
call no more if you're gonna do that horseshit rap crap. That
ridiculous shit really sets me off, man. Wait . . . *great!* Now I'm
in a bad mood because of that clown!

AX: No doubt.

JAK: *¡Ojalá que dispare llamas por el culo!*—Hopefully, flames
shoot from between his cheeks!

AX: Word. Okay, who's our next caller?

CALLER: Hi, this is Lucinda.

JAK: *Lucinda?* What do *you* want?

CALLER: You don't call me anymore, Juanny. What's going
on?

JAK: Juan's not here.

CALLER: Juanny, how come you never call me?

JAK: Who is this?

CALLER: Lucinda.

JAK: Lucinda's not here.

CALLER: Who?

JAK: Lucinda.

CALLER: Yes?

JAK: What?

AX: All right, let me step in here. *(click)* Good call. I'm glad I
wasn't listening. Who's next?

CALLER: This is Todd. My friend turned into a werezombie.

JAK: What is that?

CALLER: He must have been bitten by a zombie, because now he becomes a werezombie when the moon is full.

JAK: So, he's a werezombie at night?

CALLER: When the moon is full.

JAK: What about during the day?

CALLER: He's a cook at the cafe. Makes a decent patty melt.

JAK: Does he know he changes when there's a full moon?

CALLER: He does now cuz I told him, but he doesn't believe me. He says he's just in bed sleeping. But he doesn't realize that he changes.

JAK: So what does he do when he changes into a werezombie?

CALLER: Mostly just sleep, so far. But I have a feeling he's going to be doing a whole lot more pretty soon.

JAK: Try not to call here anymore. *(click)* Next caller.

CALLER: Hey, man, I was wondering—

AX: You've heard of a "three dog night," right?

CALLER: What? Yeah, it's a song from the seventies.

AX: You're thinking of the band—that's not what I'm talking about. Now listen, long ago in Australia, the cowboys slept outside so they could keep an eye on their animals, even in the winter. On the cold nights, they would huddle up with one of their dogs in order to keep warm; the Aborigines did the same.

CALLER: So what?

AX: Well, obviously they would say it's a "three dog night" when it was really cold and they needed more than one dog.

CALLER: What about it?

AX: We don't have any dogs, that's what.

CALLER: Neither do I. What of it?

AX: You should know: tonight's going to be a "three zombie night."

CALLER: I'm not sleeping with zombies!

AX: Your loss.

CALLER: That's sick! How's a zombie supposed to keep you warm anyway when they're cold as the grave?

AX: That's the idea.

CALLER: What idea?

AX: It's going to be very warm tonight, so I thought a couple zombies could help keep me cool and I can sleep better. See? I use their coldness against them.

CALLER: What if they attack you?

AX: Hmm . . . well, *thanks a lot!* You just ruined a perfectly good plan, jerk! *(click)* Okay, no more calls about sleeping zombies. Who's next?

CALLER: Yeah, I was gonna ask you something, but that last thing you said didn't even make any—

AX: It's a sad thing when you see a zombie stumbling and falling, unable to stay upright. You feel sorry for him because you know the reason is that he was a body parts donor. Right after he died, some doctor carved out his knee filaments and tendons and donated them to some old perv who tore up his own knees falling down the stairs in a police raid. So the sad thing is, you can call the zombie donor a hero, but no way is that crip gonna qualify for the Zombie Olympics.

CALLER: What does that—

AX: Thanks for the call, bro. *(click)*

JAK: All right, we're out of time. That's gonna do it for today, folks. I gotta go to work.

AX: Hey, Dad, before we go, did you know people are sleep-texting now? It's true—usually it's at night and they're texting back and forth and then, you know, it starts getting late and they fall asleep. But the need to text is powerful, so they keep texting, even though they're sleeping, and the messages are usually nonsense, or unintentional confessions. Anybody out there ever do that?

JAK: I slept twenty-six hours once.

AX: Texting while you're asleep is tricky, and it's leading to embarrassing text messages, as well as angry girlfriends. It's no joke, and I'll tell you this: I don't text too much, but I have gotten into the bad habit of puntexting, which is donkey-punting zombies in my sleep. It's starting to turn into a problem, I'll tell you what. You can ask Ma about that. It's gotten to the point where not a day goes by when I don't wake up in the morning and feel shame. Well, not shame, really. More like tired. Ass tired. I gotta start going to bed earlier.

JAK: I got up before I went to bed once.

AX: Hey, we had a lot of great calls today and it was fun. Thanks to everybody for their excellent questions. Keep your hands inside at all times and the zombies in your crosshairs. We'll talk to you again tomorrow.

JAK: Adios!

And that's how our first radio show went. We may have had a rough patch or two, but all in all, I think it went pretty well. The show's been on for a few months now and it's still going strong. We're trying to cut down on the violence, but you know what that's like, bro! So far we've managed to help everybody with their zombie problems, so that's cool too.

Sometimes people get upset and blame us for stuff. But we don't want to get into blaming each other, what with them blaming us and us blaming them. That's not going to solve anything. Let's just say they were wrong and peacefully let it drop.

11

NEVER PLAY WITH ZOMBIES ON A FULL STOMACH

Well, that's the end of my first notebook. Now I'm just hoping one of those Facebook guys will come around and put me on his page so I can get my story out there.

You know, people always ask me why we don't move away from the zombies, and I tell them that in order to do that, I'd have to win the lottery first. Then I'd take my winnings and start a business completely run by zombies. And probably after around three weeks, I'd quit my job as CEO of the profitable company. Two days later, I'd show up for work and ask them how it's going without me. If they said everything was fine, I'd offer to work for free and then not show up for a few days to let them know they can't boss me around.

If you have zombies, don't sweat it. For one thing, I don't see why you couldn't just round up a few of them, put 'em in a holding pen, and feed them nothing but toasted hamburger buns with pickle relish on them. And if that doesn't work, you should move to a new place. That's what I did. Problem was, I moved next door to the zombies. Don't do that—stay right where you are!

And now that I think about it, probably the only thing you can do is detain several zombies and put them on sedatives. Then when they're knocked out, cleverly place electronic ankle bracelets on them. That way, when they are released back into the wild, you can easily track their movements. And since they always stay in one place, you can watch them from the window.

Oh, and here's something you should know: if I die, I'm not going to get back up and stumble around like some loser zombie, making a skeptical of myself. Instead, I'm getting my hands on a secret map of all the uncharted zombie regions they have. Then I'm on my way to becoming the greatest ruler the zombie kingdom has ever had.

Finally, just remember that a zombie is not something you want to mess around with. You're thinking of a stink beetle. A zombie is different.

ABOUT THE AUTHOR

DONNIE SMITH is a survivor of the notorious midnight shift, where he spent several years working as a bouncer, security guard, and correctional officer. Shaped by those experiences and searching for more harrowing adventures, the obvious next step was to become an elementary schoolteacher. He earned degrees in history and education, and upon accepting his first teaching position, which was in a rural three-room elementary school, he asked his principal for the most effective instructional model for a multi-grade classroom and was told, "You'll figure it out." He did, and over the next several years he taught up to five grades simultaneously and received numerous accolades for excellence in teaching. Now a full-time author, he's working on the second book of his *Ax Handel's Special Zombie Notebooks* series, set for publication in 2014. Contact him at www.donniesmithwrites.wordpress.com and twitter.com/donniewrites.

Printed in Germany
by Amazon Distribution
GmbH, Leipzig